As S...

Child-Woman. A creature of quicksilver emotion—childlike, joyous, sulky, angry, tender, serious.

MARILYN

Sex Symbol. Worshiped by millions, with husbands and lovers following one another in her stormy, passionate life. The Love Goddess who could not succeed in marriage.

MARILYN

Legend. Struggling with ambition and pills. Going under and coming up again.

Everything that is human, Marilyn was. Her story is unending, but something is told here that has never been told before.

"Rosten's book must offer the tenderest portrait available of Monroe . . . a fine and intimate account."

—Norman Mailer

NORMAN ROSTEN, poet, playwright, and novelist, is author of *Under the Boardwalk* and *Over and Out*. He has received a Guggenheim Fellowship and an award from the American Academy of Arts and Letters. Mr. Rosten was a personal friend of Marilyn Monroe during the last seven years of her life.

Other SIGNET Books You'll Enjoy

☐ **BOGIE: The Biography of Humphrey Bogart by Joe Hyams; with an Introduction by Lauren Bacall.** BOGIE does more than report events. It relives a life. The brawls, the sprees, the razor-edged wise-cracks: Hyams describes them all. He recaptures the deep friendships—with Spencer Tracy, Judy Garland, Katharine Hepburn. He probes Bogart's stormy youth; his stubborn climb to stardom; his three rocky marital adventures and his last happy marriage to Lauren Bacall. (#Y5404—$1.25)

☐ **GEORGIA: MY LIFE IN BURLESQUE by Georgia Sothern.** Complete with 16 pages of photographs, this is the memoir of the teen-age virgin who be-came the sensational stripper queen of burlesque! "Georgia Sothern's book is the greatest show biz bio I've read in many a moon."—Mickey Spillane (#Y5287—$1.25)

☐ **SPENCER TRACY by Larry Swindell.** In this first biography ever written about the actor, we see Spencer Tracy as he really was—gruff, intensely emotional and completely honest. We see him with his cronies and his long personal and pro-fessional relationship with Katharine Hepburn. A complete listing of every film he did and an Index is included. "Meticulous portrait . . . it gives us all the dimensions . . . of a rare, real giant of yesterday's picture parade."—New York Times Book Review (#Q4486—95¢)

☐ **DO YOU SLEEP IN THE NUDE? by Rex Reed.** Rex Reed interviews Barbra Streisand, Warren Beatty, Ava Gardner, Mike Nichols, Lester Maddox, and lots of other stars—and stripping them of their public images gets down to the truth about their private lives. (#Q3773—95¢)

THE NEW AMERICAN LIBRARY, INC.,
P.O. Box 999, Bergenfield, New Jersey 07621

Please send me the SIGNET BOOKS I have checked above. I am enclosing $_____(check or money order—no currency or C.O.D.'s). Please include the list price plus 25¢ a copy to cover handling and mailing costs. (Prices and numbers are subject to change without notice.)

Name_____

Address_____

City_____State_____Zip Code_____
Allow at least 3 weeks for delivery

Marilyn:
An Untold Story

★★★★★★★★★★★★★★★★★★★★★★★★★★★★★★★★★★★★★★

by
NORMAN ROSTEN

Ⓢ

A SIGNET BOOK

NEW AMERICAN LIBRARY

TIMES MIRROR

Copyright © 1967, 1972, 1973 by Norman Rosten

All rights reserved

Poems from *Thrive Upon the Rock* by Norman Rosten © 1965
Trident Press.

 SIGNET TRADEMARK REG. U.S. PAT. OFF. AND FOREIGN COUNTRIES
REGISTERED TRADEMARK—MARCA REGISTRADA
HECHO EN CHICAGO, U.S.A.

SIGNET, SIGNET CLASSICS, SIGNETTE, MENTOR AND PLUME BOOKS
are published by The New American Library, Inc.,
1301 Avenue of the Americas, New York, New York 10019

FIRST PRINTING, SEPTEMBER, 1973

   1 2 3 4 5 6 7 8 9

PRINTED IN THE UNITED STATES OF AMERICA

I.

I left my home of green rough wood,
A blue velvet couch.
I dream till now
A shiny dark bush
Just left of the door.

Down the walk
Clickity clack
As my doll in her carriage
Went over the cracks—
"We'll go far away."

II.

Don't cry my doll
Don't cry
I hold you and rock you to sleep

Hush hush I'm pretending now
I'm not your mother who died.

III.

Help Help
Help I feel life coming closer
When all I want is to die.

      —Marilyn Monroe

1.

"... And I want to say that the people —if I am a star—the people made me a star—no studio, no person, but the people did."

She leans against a tree, her back toward me, unaware of my presence. It is summer, the air is still. Her shoulders droop with a faint suggestion of weariness that seems to envelop the entire body. Her hip touches the tree trunk, one leg slightly bent at the knee. The posture seems to suggest a deep inner loneliness. The unseen face is looking toward the field, I know her eyes are staring wistfully into space. A painter might catch these physical lines and tell the whole character. She is held in reverie for a moment. It is only after she moves that I speak.

It breaks the spell. Laughing, we go inside the house to join the others.

She sits on the beach, wearing a man's shirt over her bathing suit. We have all returned from a swim. She is listening to the conversation. We are her new friends, and she is timid with us. Her face turns from one speaker to the other, eyes revealing a curiosity in what's being said. Her eyes are warm. A radiant softness illuminates her features.

She stands at the window of her apartment, with a view of Manhattan's East River, looking out in the gray afternoon, silent, pensive. Her maid quietly ushers me into the room. Watching her, I begin a poem in my mind:

> You stand, finger at your lips, lost
> In a long-abandoned heaven . . .

She lies on the couch, asleep, her head turned to one side, hair seeming to flow back upon the pillow. Her blouse is open at the throat, an artery pulses against the pale skin. Her breathing is regular, peaceful. She is a child despite the long artificial lashes, the carefully done hair, the voluptuous body; the spirit of the child hangs over her like an innocent light. Her eyelids tremble, a dream perhaps . . . ?

Her eyes open. She answers, fully awake. "What day is it?"

She waves her hand from inside the plane as it pulls slowly away from the boarding apron. Her face is framed in the round window like a cameo. She is on her way back to California, and I had driven her to the airport. She puts her face close to the window, her lips move. Is she smiling? She seems so very fragile and alone. The plane is now turning into the approach lane leading to the take-off area, and slips away into the dusk. Her face disappears.

Years earlier, her first visit to our apartment. End of the day, a figure coming up the stairs in a camel's hair coat, no makeup, hair short and careless and wet. I watched from above as she turned into the second floor of the curving stairwell. She looked like a pretty high school kid on an errand. She stopped for a moment at the turn to allow her male companion to pass her, then followed close behind him. He was an old friend of mine, a professional photographer undoubtedly on some assignment and using the girl as a model. He had phoned half an hour earlier from a nearby park asking if he could drop in with a friend to escape the rain that had just begun. I answered yes, come on, you're both welcome.

Now they reach my landing. Photographer Sam Shaw mumbles her name; it sounds like Marion. She murmurs, "Pleased to meet you," and enters the living room, finds a chair, and sits at once, rather stiffly, but her eyes are mischievous. She snuggles into the chair with a shy smile. I notice her shoes are wet and suggest she remove them. She does. My wife Hedda enters to say hello and immediately goes out to put up some coffee. Then we chat, small talk about the weather and Brooklyn Botanical Gardens. She listens more than she speaks; the sentences are short, breathless.

She notices a slender book on a nearby table, with my name as author, entitled *Songs for Patricia,* and picks it up for examination. I explain it's a book of poems about my young daughter. Her eyes widen. She opens the pages and reads silently. Now my wife rejoins us with coffee and cake. While Sam and I are gossiping, my wife sits next to our other visitor, and I catch part of their conversation.

"No, I'm not from New York," she is saying. "I've been here for about a month. I'm studying at the Actors Studio."

"That's wonderful," replies Hedda, impressed. "Then you must have been in theater. What plays have you been in?"

"No, I've never been on the stage. But I have done some movies."

"Oh? What was your movie name?"

In a timid voice: "Marilyn Monroe."

Sam hears this and laughs. "Didn't I tell you?"

So this was the girl whose name and pictures studded the papers with increasing prominence. She had left Hollywood after a contract dispute; her latest film, *Seven Year Itch,* was a brilliant success; her recent divorce from Joe DiMaggio was still news, and here she sits—strange as it now seems—anonymous in Brooklyn.

Our first meeting did not end there. We invited

them to come along to a party in the neighborhood that same evening. Marilyn laughed merrily when I said nobody would recognize her the way she was dressed; the thought didn't bother her at all. And so, a few hours later, we walked the three blocks to the party. I introduced her with, "I'd like you to meet a friend, Marilyn Monroe." Nobody believed me. They continued to drink and talk, accepting my joke (they thought) in good spirit. Marilyn enjoyed herself, tentatively joining in the general gossip and games. During that half hour I reintroduced her to my host. "Sure," he said, "happy to meet any of your friends, even Greta Garbo."

The point was, when she entered, she did not look like Marilyn Monroe. She was totally, mysteriously, unrecognizable, as if she had stepped into the reality of her true self. She attracted them all. Everyone was soon drawn to her. Was it her voice, the half-shy, half-curious way she looked at people, her sudden warmth, that quick, infectious laugh?

Waldorf-Astoria letterhead. Undated (early 1955). Received a few days after that visit.

Dear Norman,

It feels a little funny to be writing the name "Norman" since my own name is

13

Norma and it feels like I'm writing my own name almost, however—

First, thanks for letting Sam and me visit you and Hedda on Saturday—it was nice. I enjoyed meeting your wife she was very warm to me— However, again—

Thanks the most for your book of poetry—which I spent all Sunday morning in bed with. It touched me very much—I used to think if I had ever had a child I would have wanted only a son—but after "Songs for Patricia"—I know I would have loved a little girl as much—but maybe the former feeling was only Freudian anyway or something—

I used to write poetry sometimes but usually I was depressed at those times. The few I showed it to—(in fact about two people)—said that it depressed them—one of them cried but it was an old friend I'd known for a long time.

I hope to see you again.
So anyway thanks.
And my best to Hedda and Patricia and you—

Marilyn M.

That spring seemed a happy time in her life. She had met new friends in New York; she found a new analyst; she began attending the Actors Studio and taking private acting lessons from its eminent director, Lee Strasberg. And the most crucial event: She had renewed her acquaintance with Arthur Miller to whom she had been casually introduced earlier in Hollywood.

I was driving her out to our rented summer place on the north shore of Long Island, two hours from New York. It was then, for the first time, that I realized the extent of her fame. This time, everyone recognized her. With the roof down, visible as hell, she was a blinking buoy, a sweet-sounding siren, a magnetic field. People waved and shouted from passing cars as we crossed the 59th Street Bridge. "Hi, Marilyn! Hello, Marilyn! Hey, good luck! Is that you, Marilyn? Love you!" And she waved back, sipping champagne from a paper cup. (The chilled bottle nesting in the glove compartment and several others tucked away in the trunk.)

I was grimly trying to shake these admirers.

"Cheer up," she said, laughing. "They won't hurt us."

"You mean they won't hurt *you*," I replied. "The last guy who waved looked like he wanted to lynch *me*."

The sun blazed overhead. The car sped along.

She sipped the champagne in silence, then said, "It scares me. All those people I don't know, sometimes they're so emotional. I mean if they love you that much without knowing you, they can also hate you the same way."

As a summer weekend house guest, she fitted in well with the family. On the surface, cheerful and cooperative. She helped cook, prepare spaghetti and open the clams, and always volunteered to do the dishes. She was especially proud of her dishwashing and held up the glasses for inspection, explaining she had more experience than anyone at washing dishes from the foster homes of her childhood. It was both a reminder and a disclaimer of her "waif" past. Champagne was another gesture of emancipation. Champagne and caviar were the very opposite of waifdom. Each popping cork proclaimed: Look at me, this is no abandoned child, no orphan!

She played badminton with a real flair, once banging friend Ettore Rella on the head (no damage). She was relaxed, giggling, tender.

She liked her guest room; she'd say, nodding for the shade to be drawn at bedtime, "Make it dark and give me air." She slept late, got her own breakfast, and went off for a walk in the woods with only the cat for company.

Her summer visits were not always restful. Everywhere she went, there was a potential scene.

Because anything could happen with her around, wherever it was. Explosion. No match, just her and air. Spontaneous combustion. We had some close calls. One of these still gives me a small sweat to this day. (In retrospect, all adventures with Marilyn had this unpredictable, ominous side, as though she were thumbing her nose at fate. She and fate always seemed to be side-stepping one another; I think fate was a little scared of her.)

It happened on the beach. Deserted area. Small group, big umbrella. Champagne from the trunk compartment of the car, neatly packed in dry ice. I will not attempt to describe her bathing suit except to say I have a photo of her in that suit I look at when the poetry is going bad and I need a charge.

Two stringy boys, idly paddling by in a camp canoe, saw her, edged closer for a look, and sped away with the news. As though a colony of ants had been activated, teen-agers began to file past us, first in wide circles around our party, then moving in closer, and finally about fifty worshipers converged upon the umbrella under which she demurely sat. She rose to greet them.

"Hey, Marilyn, I see all your movies!"

"You're my favorite!"

"You look terrific!"

"Marilyn, how about a kiss!"

She shook their hands and joked with them.

They brought stones for her to autograph. The boys circled her tightly, the girls screamed, and a kind of panic set in. They reached for her with wild little cries, touching her, uttering pleas, begging favors while she laughed, fended them off as they slowly crowded her toward the water. Finally, the only escape was the water, and with an apprehensive wave, she started swimming. A barrage of cheers, and fifty tanned young bodies plunged in and gave chase.

Several of our group swam after her, trying to cut them off. They kept clamoring for Marilyn; she was surrounded.

"Hey," she called to me faintly. "Get me out of here!"

I managed to plough through to her side, shouting at the kids: "Beat it, get moving, go on home!" I struck at them blindly, furiously, and seizing her by the arm, started swimming out into deeper water. I threatened those hardier ones who followed; they watched us, grinning, as we plodded out.

Suddenly, Marilyn stopped.

"I can't swim any more," she pleaded.

"What do you mean, you can't."

"I'm not a good swimmer even when I'm good," she said.

"We can't turn back. Those vultures are waiting."

"You go back and let me die."

I saw the headlines: FILM STAR DROWNED. FRIEND IN FUTILE RESCUE ATTEMPT. SUICIDE PACT HINTED. She was breathing hard, her chin just above the water. "Listen," I said. "Can you float? Try it. Take a deep breath and lean back." She tried but swallowed water and began to cough. I circled her, puffing a bit, and attempted to get her to lie back on the water. "Boy, what a way to go!" she gasped, clutching me. I thought of yelling for help, but if those kids swam out to help us, we'd drown for sure.

How else would we be saved if not by a Hollywood ending? The roar of a motor boat on the soundtrack. Real boat on wide-screen water. This crew-cut kid snakes up alongside, idles the motor. We both grabbed on to the side. I climbed into the boat, and there was the problem of hauling M. up over the side. She was rather dead weight by now, and she was not then nor had she ever been a thin slip of a girl. I finally pulled her up, and she fell heavily into the boat.

I looked at her as she lay exhausted, her legs curled up, her pink toes gleaming in the sun. The boy-pilot also regarded her with an adolescent's transfixed stare, forgetting the wheel and executing two tight circles before I realized what was happening. I shouted at him, and she said, "Don't be nervous, it's a wonderful weekend!"

That was the only time I had the chance to save her life.

She could give an appearance of toughness, and she could be tough. She knew the price—and paid it—of living in a professional world and industry dominated by men. She was engaged in a struggle to be herself. In the film industry women were chattel, packaged sex, decoys for the gullible public. On more than one occasion, Marilyn showed her independence. When she posed for the famous nude calendar—very daring in the early fifties—she defended it on the grounds that (1) she had to pay her rent, and it was honest work, and (2) the human body is nothing to be ashamed of (a sentiment that was to become the battle cry of Women's Liberation a decade later).

At the height of her fame, she was approached to model for a TV bra commercial. She turned it down contemptuously; she knew the difference between necessity and exploitation. But she had no qualms about wearing a dress without a stitch beneath it. One summer in the country, Hedda and she went shopping in Saks Fifth Avenue (Southampton). Marilyn was wearing a simple white cotton dress. A saleslady recognized her and with barely restrained excitement selected a half-dozen dresses for Marilyn to try on. In the dressing room the effusive saleslady said, "Let me help you," and unzipped the back of her dress, which fell to the floor. There stood Marilyn like Venus rising from that famous half shell. The saleslady, flustered, blushed. "Oh dear," she murmured, wondering perhaps if it was against the rules to try on Saks gowns over a nude body—even this famous one. But Marilyn blithely proceeded to try them. Perhaps because she noticed the saleslady's concern, she bought all six.

I suspect she would have quarreled with her sisters on the sex-liberation issue. In terms of economic equality with men, she had long proved herself. Certainly her problems in finding herself went far beyond and much deeper than the emancipation promises of Women's Liberation. She was very aware of herself as a woman and enjoyed her femininity, recognizing very well its power over others. However narcissistic or exhibitionist her feelings about herself, they were corroborated daily by the media and the masses of her admirers. Many women were drawn to her, probably more keenly aware than men of her extreme vulnerability; nor did they see her as a threat.

Marilyn sensed the difference in sexual psychology between men and women. She would tell of the time in Hollywood when Khrushchev, the Soviet premier, was being honored at a dinner. She was seated at a table in the audience (her studio had "demoted" her from the VIP dais) when Khrushchev passed by to shake her hand. "He didn't say anything," Marilyn recounted with pride. "He just looked at me. He looked at me the way a man looks on a woman. That's how he looked at me."

Marilyn was a true seductress. She didn't want to be considered a sex symbol or any symbol, but she enjoyed her role as a sexual person. She would laugh and say that to her a "cymbal" was something in an orchestra. She was an individual, and a woman. If men whistled at her, that was OK; if they were obscene, she knew how to handle it. She understood the carnal male syndrome and would never censure a man for beating the woman to the draw, so to speak. She enjoyed the idea of men desiring her; it amused, flattered, and excited her. She needed that proof of being adored; it denied the inner dread of being unwanted, the trauma of the illegitimate and motherless child. She sensed love as the hidden miracle in the human scheme. Love the great equalizer—if one were lucky enough to find it.

She searched everywhere—in life and in books. What she lacked in formal education she made up for in curiosity and a kind of unschooled knowledge. When she talked about books she had read or liked, her enthusiasm bubbled over. When she got on the Dostoevski kick and suggested publicly she'd like to play Grushenka in the movie version of *The Brothers Karamazov*, the literary snob set had their big laugh. It didn't bother her. They thought she was kooky; she thought they were phony. They couldn't understand that she was serious. (At another news conference, when she indicated a desire to do a Broadway play, a reporter threw the words at her: *"Brothers Karamazov?"* Unruffled, Marilyn replied patiently, "I don't want to play the brothers. I want to play Grushenka; that's a girl's part." How do you spell Grushenka? "Well, it starts with a G" was her answer.)

She liked poetry. It was a short cut for her. She understood, with the instinct of a poet, that it led directly into the heart of experience. She knew the interior floating world of the poem with its secrets, phantoms, and surprises. She loved surprises, verbal or visual. She enjoyed mischief and mystery, things a good poem can give. And somewhere within her, she sensed a primary truth: that poetry is allied with death. Its intoxication and joy are the other face of elegy. Love and death, opposite and one, are its boundary—and were hers.

One evening at our house with friends, someone suggested an impromptu poetry reading. The idea was to pass around a copy of Whitman and Yeats, each to open a page at random and read. At Marilyn's turn, she opened the Yeats, and the poem could only have been presented to her, again, by fate. It was "Never Give All the Heart." ("For everything that's lovely is/But a brief, dreamy, kind delight./O never give the heart outright . . .") She read the title, paused, and began the poem. She read it slowly, discovering it, letting the lines strike her, surprised, hanging on, winning by absolute simplicity and truth.

When she finished, there was a hush. She stared into space.

You'd never know when she'd phone in the middle of the night without identifying herself, her voice low, breathless, impossible to disguise. "Hello, it's me. What's everybody doing?" And you'd say, "My God, Marilyn, it's 2 A.M. Everybody's asleep." She'd apologize. "I'm sorry. I thought we could stir up some mischief. Well, some other time. Say g'night to all." And she'd hang up. Or phone at 3 A.M. from California (midnight there), waking the house with a bright "Happy birthday!" You'd grumble at the hour, and she'd say she was sorry. You had to be on her time. She never got the time thing straightened out: It was a built-in, psychic time, Marilyn time. Possibly Einstein time. (He was one of her pinups.) In a sense, these calls reassured her, placed her in relation to time. Filling up time in the nightmare of aloneness.

In those early days of her residence in New York—between husbands and a new career—my wife and I would sometimes accompany her to the theater or a concert. On one occasion, I alone escorted her to a concert. (I was a safe, nonrecognizable, nongossip companion.) It sounds glamorous; it also was hard work. There we were one night, seated in Carnegie Hall, she in her devastating dress, I in my assembly-line suit, waiting for the great Russian pianist Emil Gilels to enter onstage and be seated at the piano. "Relax," she whispered with that little laugh of hers. "They don't know who you are." True. But while everyone was staring at her, their eyes were sweeping over me as well. Conflicting emotions of escape and recognition brought on a sudden pallor. She leaned toward me. "Don't be nervous. You're doing great."

I don't know if word of her presence got backstage, but Gilels played like a man inspired. At intermission, a Carnegie official approached and informed us that Mrs. Gilels was seated in a box across from our part of the dress circle and asked to meet her. Marilyn took my hand (she was worried I'd back out), and with half of the hall watching, we crossed over to the box where Mrs. Gilels was chatting with a short, intense man. It was Gilels himself. Marilyn introduced me as "my poet friend," and I tried my best to look poetic. He said to her, "You must visit Russia one day. Everyone would like to see you." She answered, "I would love to, and some day I will. Right now I'm reading Dostoevski." Then she turned to Mrs. Gilels, who didn't seem to know more than a dozen words of English. "He's a great man, your husband, you must be so proud of him." Mrs. G. smiled sweetly. It was a high moment in international relations.

Out in the street, the crowd surges around us. "Don't leave me," she whispers, but we are separated. Luckily, someone guides her to a waiting taxi. Shall I flee or follow? The crush is unending. She calls to me. I fight my way inside the cab.

She is ambivalent about crowds. Multiplied, they become an audience of millions, tens of millions—in a sense, her life. But individuals who make up the crowd regress, and they can be unpredictable, even violent. They follow her, wait in doorways, shout at her, leap after her into taxis, keep watch on the street below her window. They send letters—imploring, demanding, weeping, threatening—the mad or bewitched seekers. They ask for autographs, money, photos, articles of her clothing. They propose marriage or trysts, find her phone number and use obscenities.

The crowd, at the theater or a concert, moves around her, moves away and closes in behind her as she passes, a tide of living men and women who smell out the one they will later crucify. They invariably pick a magical talisman: contradictory, all-embracing, wife-mother-mistress, the mysterious link between sex and death. For as certain as they adore her, they could also destroy her.

She played a game with the crowd, a teasing game of hide-and-seek. She would go through the ritual of disguise: glasses, sloppy dress, long scarf, no makeup or a mask makeup, flat shoes, outlandish hat. She wanted to be disguised and discovered simultaneously. She would hire a huge limousine, and if that wasn't enough to attract attention, she would draw the shades. Was Marilyn challenging the crowd to pierce the cover and recognize the true persona? The thrill of the stranger saying, "I know who you are!"

It was a self-defeating game. As soon as she took two steps, Marilyn announced herself.

I had mentioned the Rodin section at the Metropolitan Museum of Art, knowing it would delight her, and for months she promised to see it. But these were busy months devoted to decisions affecting her career and personal life.

One day the phone rang. "It's me," said the breathless voice. "I'm ready, C. B., if you are!" The perfect Monroe sentence: timeless, directionless.

I asked, "Ready for what? And where? Not to mention with whom?"

"The Rodin. You promised, remember? I'm free this afternoon. If you're free, that is."

And so, that very afternoon, we met at the museum. She wore one of her "disguises"—dark glasses, crazy hat, no makeup, a loose coat to decurve her—but the Rodin wing was relatively empty. We wandered inside a world of breathing marble.

Two pieces fascinated her: "Pygmalion" and "The Hand of God." "The Hand of God" depicts

in dazzling white marble a huge hand curving up-
ward in which a man and a woman are entwined
in an embrace of lyricism and passion. They are
together and apart. The woman's hair streams
from the stone. Marilyn walked around and
around that small white miracle, her eyes wide as
she removed her dark glasses.

One morning, a call from a friend. "Did you
see the paper? You made Walter Winchell's
column! Where else can you go but down, haha."

I got the *Daily Mirror*. There it was, the first
sentence in the gossip chart of the day:

MARILYN MONROE IS COOING IT IN POETRY WITH
NORMAN ROSTEN.

Wow. Should I laugh or groan? My wife
laughed. "I like the word 'cooing,'" she said. "It's
certainly better than 'wooing.'"

Marilyn phoned, very upset. "Did you see the
Winchell?"

"I've memorized it."

"Listen, I don't know how it got there. I hope
you're not embarrassed by it. Please don't be.
God, what an idiot that man is!" A pause.
"Hedda isn't mad at me?"

"No."

"I'm glad." She let out a sharp breath. "Jesus,
that's how I lose friends. I'm sorry about it."

"Look, Marilyn, it doesn't bother me if it

doesn't bother you. If the great Winchell says we're cooing, he should know, right?"

"Right, that dummy!" She laughed hysterically.

"As we were."

"Still friends?"

"Still."

She sighed. "Can I speak to Hedda?"

I knew the girls were going to enjoy this talk.

She was already a favorite of the columnists—Winchell, Earl Wilson, Maurice Zolotow, and others. Her wit and/or naïveté made good copy. "What have you got on, Marilyn?" a reporter is reported to have asked over the phone. Reply: "Nothing but the radio."

Other examples (from an Earl Wilson interview in 1955).

Q: Is it true you wear one thing to bed—Chanel No. 5?

A: I like to wear something different once in a while. Now and then I switch to Arpege.

Q: Do you have any love interest now?

A: No. No serious interests . . . but I'm always interested.

(It wasn't just zaniness or naïveté; often a serious thrust in her reply would simply demolish the cliché question. When Miller came into the picture, she was asked what attracted her to this man. She answered: "Everything . . . Haven't you seen him?")

"Hey, would you and Hedda come to dinner? I'm trying a new dish."

She was practicing cooking. My wife and I would sometimes come by at her apartment and be dutiful food testers. Cookbook stuff mostly. Stews. Wild omelettes. Roast beef. I remember a stunning bouillabaisse. Salads of strange ingredients: sometimes lettuce with oil and no vinegar, while I swear once it was all vinegar with shreds of lettuce. Or sauce with meat instead of meat with sauce. However, she was very good at desserts, and her color schemes (peas and carrots), if not striking, managed to be consistent.

At one time, in Manhattan alone, she lured me up to be the guinea pig. Poets are always hungry, more or less. And I didn't mind.

"You're a real friend to do this," she said, using pepper and salt and dill weed and God knows what else on a simmering dish. "How does it taste?"

"Uh, well . . ."

"Too spicy?"

"Yes, now that you mention it."

"Oh, dear. Let me tone it down."

She held a small humming sort of machine

over the steaming bowl. "I'm cooling it off," she said.

"What the hell is that thing?"

"A portable hair dryer."

My birthday (January first) would sometimes get a short note from her:

Dear Norman,

Happy Birthday, Happy New Year, Happy, Happy. Also I owe you one letter and one poem.

Or sometimes a regular card, one with the inscription:

I mean I'm so glad you were born and I'm living at the same time as you

Love,

Noodle, Sam,

Max, Clump,

Sugar Finny, Pussy,

and all the rest of us

She owned a beautiful russet striped cat, female, who had unaccountably become pregnant in a high-rise city apartment dwelling (a hallway romance?). Marilyn got wildly involved in the pregnancy, reading up on the subject, watching over

the cat, feeding her extra delicacies, etc. She
would interrupt a business session or evening on
the town to call her maid and check on kitty. She
counted the days, studied every sign, became nervous as the event approached. She had a box
prepared with a soft blanket. There was never a
more spoiled prenatal cat in feline history. She'd
phone in daily bulletins: Cat looked fine, cat
seemed to be breathing hard, cat didn't eat much,
cat looked listless or looked crazy. And all the
while wondering how dear cat got pregnant, it
wasn't fair, animals were so helpless sexually, and
what did I think? I thought if those kittens didn't
arrive soon, I would get an unlisted phone. And
then, D-day, Delivery, well past midnight (even
with cats, it seems), the phone ringing, and her
breathless voice, "They're coming, the kittens!
Hurry, take a cab!" Let it be known that I played
this scene with masculine calm. "Name one after
me," I said, and hung up quietly, then went back
to sleep.

The courtship of Miller and Monroe was surrounded by the circus of politics—that era of
witch-hunting in the fifties when Sen. Joseph
McCarthy and Rep. Francis J. Walter of the Sen-
ate Internal Security Committee and House Committee on Un-American Activities prowled the
landscape for victims. And headlines. It was a
time of cowardice on a national scale. Strong citi-

zens fell before the rhetoric of pygmies; dignified men groveled and wept. To be called a communist or communist sympathizer ("fellow traveler") was tantamount to treason. A comic opera with real bodies all over the place.

Arthur Miller was accused of having connections with the Communist Party. Nothing was proved. Nothing had to be proved. The statement was enough; indictment by the media followed. But love was waiting in the wings. The gossip columns throughout America had for many months been planted with rumors that Miller and Monroe were romantically involved; more than that, the word "marriage" began to appear, denied of course by both parties. Still, the pot was bubbling. America panted with fantasies of the Brain versus the Body; all the submerged sex of the nation rose to the surface.

Miller was called to testify before the House (Walter) Committee. Marilyn, against the frantic advice from her studio (she still owed 20th Century several films), went down to Washington on a brief visit to give Miller moral support, appearing with him publicly, then returning while he waited to go before the Committee.

In his appearance, while discussing his own political associations freely (flatly denying Communist Party membership), he refused on grounds of conscience to name other persons associated with "communist-writer's groups." Proclaimed Representative Walter, "I don't see how we can consistently not cite him because he very obviously is in contempt." At what proved to be a historic session, Miller was queried on why he had applied for a passport to visit England during the coming summer of 1956.

"What is your objective in going to England?" Committee Counsel asked.

"My objective is double," replied Miller. "I wish to attend a production of my play, and to be with the woman who will then be my wife."

Bombshell. Consternation. The image of the dangerous writer had been suddenly transformed to that of the lover.

Even Marilyn was taken by surprise. She called us, her voice breathless, high, a bit on the hysterical side. "Have you heard? He announced it before the whole world! He told the whole world he was marrying Marilyn Monroe. Me! Can you believe it? You know he never really asked me. We talked about it, but it was all very vague." Her voice raced on, "I mean, really ask *me* to marry *him!* You've got to come down right away, both of you. I need moral support. I mean, help! I'm surrounded here, locked in my apartment. There are newspapermen trying to get in, crawling all over the place, in the foyer, in the halls. I told the elevator men to let you through.

They know who you are. There's to be a press conference at 7:30. I'm supposed to make a statement."

"It's almost nine now," I groaned, thinking of the mob of newspapermen. "Where's Arthur?"

"He won't get back from Washington till later tonight. Hurry. Please. I need all the friends I have!"

When we arrived at her apartment house, we had difficulty breaking through the crowds. We reached the lobby. The press conference was in full swing. Marilyn was cornered, barely visible. We heard her saying in answer to a question: "He never had to propose to me. It was simultaneous, a simultaneous feeling that overcame us both!"

When the smoke cleared on Capitol Hill, both the Committee and the smart media realized they could not prosecute love. If Miller was going to marry Marilyn Monroe, he couldn't be all that bad. A communist could not court and win America's sweetheart, and if he did, she was certain to reform him. Romance versus the evil of totalitarianism—a perfect script. Love had indeed, like in the movies, conquered all. Marilyn made everything else appear trivial.

Congressman Walter, up for re-election, now added a touch of farce. He requested to be photographed with Miss Monroe. Request denied.

The wedding of Marilyn Monroe and Arthur Miller took place on July 1 with much secrecy at the country home of Miller's agent and friend Kay Brown. It was billed as the marriage of the century. It lasted five years.

What attracted them to one another? Why did the Brain want to marry the Body? What did the sexy blonde want from the ascetic-looking writer? What? Why? How? Answers have been given or guessed at all over the world, in huts and palaces, fashioned out of gossip and psychiatric theorizing. Of course, we shall never know; the forces that bring people together are mysterious enough, but people who are also symbols bring into play additional forces, social and psychological, that obscure any easy analysis.

One thing was clear: Miller was in love, completely, seriously, with the ardor of a man released. His first marriage had ended badly; now his second chance had come, and it swept him into channels of newly discovered emotion. It was wonderful to behold. He was happy and full of hope for the future. He even began to write poetry—thus do the gods drive even Pulitzer Prize winners mad.

Marilyn, too, blossomed with this new love. She was more beautiful than ever, in a way more unreal, as though the once-forbidden triumph had somehow transformed her into a different creature, more ethereal, more poignant.

On this day, all was serene and sunny. The day everywhere spoke of life: the long table behind the house with guests seated and drinking, bride and groom moving among friends, everyone exchanging good wishes and embraces. The bride was both beautiful and nervous. Really ecstatic. She gave off a luminosity like the Rodin marble; she was the girl in "The Hand of God." It was the culmination of a dream and carried within it the danger of all dreams.

I was to be the best man, but a relative bumped me at the last moment and got the assignment.

I said to her, "How come you're marrying that guy? He wears glasses, and his teeth are crooked."

"Oh, he's beautiful," she breathed softly.

"I always thought some day you'd run off with *me*."

She laughed. "I know men like you. You'd never leave your wife!" We kissed.

Miller came up and said, "Hey, cut that out."

"One more," I said.

"Just one!"

"I'll cook noodles like your mother," she said, clinging to him.

"Leave my mother out of it." He was getting crocked, as was everybody else.

The ceremony, performed by Rabbi Robert Goldberg, went very smoothly. Weeks before the ceremony, he had coached the bride-to-be in the

ritual of formally becoming a Jew. She participated with touching seriousness. Those who had
secretly laughed at or mocked her desire to adopt
the Jewish faith were moved to silence. That Miller did not himself come from an orthodox reli-
gious family nor was in any sense religiously committed did not in the least deflect her enthusiasm.
The desire of the foster child to be taken into the
bosom of a larger family—to belong—seemed a
worthwhile enough motive. Still, one could not
help but observe the unreality of her conversion.
Was it another game for her? A psychic toy?
There was no reason, actually, to take this step. It
just didn't make sense to me. But what made sense
to her was quite a different thing.

Marilyn rehearsed her role and was ready with
her lines. Observing the ancient Jewish ritual, she
lifted the veil to sip from a goblet of wine. She
spoke her "I do" in a clear if shaky voice, exchanged
rings, was kissed by the groom, and then received dozens of kisses by some twenty-five
friends, relatives, and a few reporters. A giddy,
delirious day. It was a fairy tale come true. The
Prince had appeared, the Princess was saved.

2.

"... *But everybody is always tugging at you. They'd all like sort of a chunk of you. They kind of like take pieces out of you.*"

Within a week, the newlywed Millers arrived in London where Marilyn was soon to begin her costarring film with Laurence Olivier, *The Prince and the Showgirl*. A tumultuous airport welcome that surprised even the British. Marilyn never seemed happier.

Their residence was one of the more modest stately homes of England, located in Englefield Green, an hour from London and an hour's drive to the studios where Marilyn was to begin work. It contained a dozen rooms, a staff of six or seven, several acres of lush green lawn, inimitable English rose gardens, and its back yard was enclosed by an iron fence and a gate that opened on Windsor Park, the private property of Her Majesty the Queen. They had the privilege of walking, bicycling, or riding on its ancient lanes and pathways. The huge trees that shaded the front of the house served to hide photographers with telescopic lenses aimed at the master-bedroom windows, hoping for an unsuspecting glimpse of the newlyweds. It was a pleasure to learn that several fell from these same trees. In England, Marilyn and Arthur Miller were, if that is possible, a bigger story than at home.

Marilyn would rise at five in the morning—the first one up, everyone else sleeping soundly—and wouldn't even bother to wake the maid for coffee. She was driven to Pinewood Studio by her chauffeur and accompanied always by a personal bodyguard. At the studio she had breakfast, and preparation for the day's shooting was begun. A couple of hours were needed for makeup, the elaborate coiffure the film required, and costumes. Marilyn was excited, determined to do her best.

But the Olivier-Monroe team proved less dazzling than had been predicted. The great classical actor and the Hollywood comedienne, he from Olympus, she from Sunset Boulevard, brought together by the God of Casting (or the Angel of Economics). It was a love-hate thing from the start, and it couldn't have happened to two nicer people from show-biz land. She respected him but suspected the feeling wasn't mutual.

That first important vibration was bad. It occurred on the opening day at the studio where the cast gathered with director Olivier preparatory to the beginning of shooting. Seated around the table were Marilyn and a group composed of some of the most brilliant actors of stage and screen. These included Dame Sybil Thorndike and Anton Walbrook. Olivier formally welcomed the company;

he expressed his delight to be working together with so many old friends. They were familiar with each other, they knew and understood the problems, he looked forward to the work ahead. He then introduced Marilyn. He remarked that it would be a new experience for her and would probably take her a while to get accustomed to their way of doing things. He was outwardly polite and gracious, but his slight smile, his change in tone from one of clubby professionalism when speaking to the rest of the cast (with whose members he had often worked) to one of careful, almost elementary explanation when speaking to Marilyn—it may have been little more than a nuance—came across to her as patronizing: he was talking down to her, she was just another Hollywood blonde. The die was cast. She was on guard from that moment: suspicious, sullen, defensive, with flashes of anger breaking out.

In the early stages of shooting, Olivier was undiplomatic enough to suggest that Marilyn's teeth came out a bit yellow in the rushes and hinted that baking soda and lemon would whiten them. She was furious at the suggestion; no one had ever complained about those perfect teeth before. Nor did the presence of husband Arthur Miller help matters between them. Further, acting coach Paula Strasberg's teachings were in conflict with the discipline and methods of an English company. Olivier became impatient, edgy, martyred;

he simply did not know how to deal with her. And Marilyn never forgave him. Once she made a judgment in relation to people, she was adamant (one of her less appealing traits); further, she demanded the loyalty of her friends in this judgment. "If you're my friend, you can't like anyone I dislike" was her motto. Things got bad enough to require the presence of Marilyn's New York analyst who flew over a number of times to try to keep her patient on an even keel during this difficult period.

Despite the chaos, Sybil Thorndike noted later that although Marilyn seemed to be doing nothing at all during the shooting, when she appeared on the screen it was a revelation. Dame Sybil was one of the few in the company who understood and appreciated this American girl. Olivier tried to reach out to her after a bad beginning, but it was already too late; Marilyn no longer trusted him.

The difficulties mounted. Behind the scenes a struggle was taking place, with producer Milton Greene, Miller, and the Strasbergs fighting for influence and control of Marilyn's future career, each believing that he was the one who could offer her the most and protect her. Miller was plunged into a world of daily crises, unspoken antagonisms, endless decisions, and with these new tensions came the necessity of providing Marilyn with almost constant support. It was a difficult, perhaps impossible, role for him.

Upon their return to the States toward the end of the year (1956), a change was discernible in Marilyn. The tone of the marriage had changed. Something new and mysterious had arisen between them, which close friends would recognize. The honeymoon cruise was over, the real voyage had begun. Storm and heartbreak ahead.

But America needed the dream. At this moment, six months after the marriage, a columnist wrote, "I don't give it six months. I don't give it six years. I give it forever."

Summer of 1957. Amagansett, Long Island. We're a few miles down the road, and Marilyn loves to bicycle over during the afternoon. Sometimes Miller accompanies her, more often she's alone. We sit around and talk, she plays games with our daughter and the cat. She appears in good spirits; we're getting used to her sudden shifts in mood. When she's high, a sweet chime of music surrounds her; when she's low, she moves to another plane, withdrawn, private.

The Millers do not socialize much. The world, however, continually intrudes. Journalists, foreign and domestic, poke around. Miller has a tough time working. I remember a morning when a helicopter descended on the field adjoining their house and whisked Marilyn off to . . . where?

Some pictorial event or other, a stunt or benefit, it wouldn't matter; she was wanted and she responded.

One evening, we gave a dinner party at our cottage. After food, there was dancing and quite a bit of merriment. Marilyn left the room at one point without a word to anyone. I followed several moments later and discovered her on the porch sobbing quietly.

"What is it, dear?" I asked, sitting next to her.

She hurriedly dried her eyes. "I can't tell you. I feel terrible, maybe it's the weather." She was plainly evasive.

"Why don't you come in and dance?"

"Well, maybe a little later."

"I don't want to leave you here to cry." What the hell else could I say?

She sniffed, straightened her hair. "Make believe I just was out here powdering my nose or something, OK? Arthur will only get upset."

"Right," I nodded. We went back inside.

Some weeks later, Marilyn was rushed by ambulance to a New York hospital because of a miscarriage—an ectopic pregnancy. We visited her. She was resting easily, but her cheerfulness didn't fool anybody.

Whatever the reasons, her inability to have a child was to loom as a crucial disappointment in her life. The love goddess, the woman supreme, unable to create a baby; it was a dagger at her ego. There was something wrong with her, inside her, a defect, an evil. Nor would pills erase this sense of failure. Despite all, she yearned to be a mother, even if it meant temporarily putting films aside. She desperately wanted fulfillment.

Marilyn had enough of the child within her to be acutely conscious of the needs of children. She knew when they were happy or withdrawn; her own childhood taught her that. She was generous with them, especially so with our daughter Patricia. She was always giving her little gifts. The nicest of these was a dog named Cindy. Marilyn had found the animal in the country, starved and barely able to walk. She nursed the dog back to health with the aid of a local veterinarian and gave her to Pat on her birthday.

She knew, too, how to be playful with children. At one time Pat, during a visit, stumbled upon Marilyn's makeup box in the bedroom. Marilyn asked, "Would you like me to make you up like sixteen?" It was an invitation young girls of ten or eleven must dream of then and now and forever. She sat my daughter in front of her huge lighted mirror and began the transformation: face rouge, lipstick, eyebrow paint, eye shadow, every beauty trick in the book. She then skillfully arranged the hair and created a smashing hairdo; she knew what made a girl attractive at any age. Pat was transfixed. Finally, satisfied with her handiwork, Marilyn stepped back and said, "Now go into the living room and show 'em!"

In New York, Marilyn met people of the theater—writers, actors, directors—and immersed herself in study and work. She hoped to become more than a star or a personality. It was her intense desire to develop as an artist and win the respect of her peers. She enjoyed her classes at the Actors Studio under the eye of Lee Strasberg. The theater then was a shining light for ambition and talent; if one made it there, one seemed to reach an elevation of art not accorded to film folk—a curious myth cherished by those who could overlook the tawdry commercialism of show biz while basking in a lost tradition of "purity."

Marilyn loved to talk about the Studio, especially as it related to her acting studies. She was very serious in the way actors can be about themselves. Her thoughts may have been feedback from class discussions or possibly certain insights of her own. I remember their vividness.

"I must try not to hide the things happening to me when I do an exercise. The thing is not to let the actress worry and let the character worry," she said one evening as she talked about a scene in class. "You have to learn to believe in the contradictory impulses, you know, you want to do one thing and you do another, you learn from that.

But basically, you find your own way from your own experience looking around you."

These new ideas excited her. In her film acting, Marilyn went more or less by instinct; now she was trying to get to theory. Groping is perhaps a better word. "... Like, for example, in this scene, how does this girl go to sleep, what does she think about? You think about someone that you feel that way about or at least similar. Another thing is to let yourself go, the pleasure of physical movement is so important. If that's a problem, you say to yourself, What is there I'm afraid of, or hiding? Maybe my libido." She thinks for a moment, and laughs. "Lee makes you think, he relates your work to your life so that you can use your life onstage. The other day we discussed the approach to a scene. Lee says it's like opening a bottle. You try different ways if it doesn't seem to open, maybe try another bottle, even many other bottles . . ." Her voice trails off, drifting with the idea. After a moment she continues, "I have to begin to face my problem in my work, and life . . . the question of how or why can I act, of which I'm not sure, because no one has experienced or known how it was in even a slightest detail, the torture let alone the day-to-day happenings . . ."

Yes, the naïve, unschooled girl is going to school, is cramming her mind with thoughts. Her desire to learn is intense. The scoffers (then and now) are always there, still doubting that the

Body could have a Mind. She did, and stayed with it out of the compulsion that is the handmaiden of art.

When she and Miller were away in the country, I'd sometimes use their apartment during the summer when I came into the city. And Marilyn would once in a while leave a sweet note.

Dear Norman,

There is a homemade strawberry short cake in the Fridge, Also milk—help yourself.

Also, however long you need to be here—1 wk—2 wks etc. feel free to come and go as you please . . .

You are not imposing. We're glad you're aboard—even if we go down—sinking—the more the merrier!

I'm leaving you with this stanza (from an unchildlike childhood)—

Here goes—
Good nite
Sleep tight
and Sweet repose
Where ever you lay your Head—
I hope you find your nose—

Marilyn

Or she'd send a short memo:

Claude [after Claude Rains whom she insisted I resembled] please take the car to the country when you go—its just hanging around the garage getting rusty . . .

Also—yes, my ankles are better and about my knees—since nothing was wrong with them—they are still okay.

Hedda—please call me when your in town, I'd love to see you— Come up to my place to rest when your spending the day in the city or we could eat or do something— what-ever you want.

Patty please give Bam-moo [the dog] and Candy [the cat with a new litter] and all her children a hug for me.

Marilyn

Norman Mailer, friend, bon vivant, and otherwise observer of the cultural scene, expressed a keen interest in Marilyn and asked me to set up a meeting with her, formal or otherwise. She resisted his approach: She was "busy," or she "had nothing to say," or "he's too tough."

"Come on," I urged her. "He's the nicest ogre you'll ever meet."

"I read his books. I haven't time for any more writers."

"He's a sincere admirer of yours," I'd insist.

"OK. And I'm an admirer of his, so we're even."

"He's soft-spoken, tenderhearted, and just wants to breathe in your perfume."

She laughed. "Yeah, that's what I'm afraid of, you writers stealing my perfume. Well, maybe I'll ask him to a party."

She did ask. But Mailer was away and out of contact. It was a meeting I had fully intended to sit in on. Fate would have it otherwise.

The Millers were giving a small party at their apartment on 57th Street, Manhattan. It included the usual champagne and dancing. Marilyn loved to dance, and Miller, too (with a few drinks), would attempt an eerie loping foxtrot, perilously off-balance, in the true party spirit. Marilyn wore a stunning dress (she was "trying it out") which, as the saying goes, she was poured into. It hung clinging and very fluid, the closest to liquid clothes I had ever seen.

She and I went into the kitchen for more ice cubes, and there was Hugo under the table. Hugo was a dog. Marilyn, on her knees, crooned tenderly to him while he, the saddest-looking basset hound in captivity, stared up at her, uttering little grumpy noises. "He's depressed," she said. "Is it possible dogs get depressed the same as people?" I nodded without a reply. Hugo never liked me from the beginning. True lover that he was, he suspected me of trying to take his mistress away from him, which was untrue. He regarded me more dourly than ever on this day. "Did you know I spoke to my doctor about Hugo?" she continued. "My doc also has a dog that acts dopey once in a while. He told me a dog can be cheered up by giving him a small shot of whiskey. What do you think?"

"A doggy martini?"

She laughed. "No. Just a teaspoon of straight Scotch."

"It can't hurt. It might improve his bark."

"Dear, dear Hugo," she mused. Then she got up. "Would you help me? Let's give it to him now. I can't bear to see him so unhappy. I mean, if the doc said so . . ."

"How can I help? I don't trust the dog. He'll nip me. Nipped by a dog taking a nip!"

"Don't you like Hugo?" She regarded me sadly.

"I do. But he belongs to you. He's your problem."

"Are you a friend?" (The test!)

"I am. You know that."

"Well, then, if I hold Hugo, would you feed him the Scotch?"

It was difficult, almost impossible, to refuse.

Marilyn easily coaxed Hugo into her lap. "Now, Hugo, dear, we want you to be happy. The doctor said this will be good for you. Good dog." She crooned while I, part of the plot, found a teaspoon, found the bottle of booze, and held the teaspoon poised for delivery. She got Hugo to yawn. On her signal, I deftly tipped the spoon into Hugo's mouth. She quickly put him down.

Hugo stood stock still, swallowed, coughed, sneezed, hurried under the table, hesitated, sat down, then rose again, wobbled a bit, and suddenly, rapturously, pattered across the room. He turned, startled, seemed to smile, and did a jog back again to where he started. He executed what appeared to be an antic pirouette, and at this point Marilyn got down on her knees, hugged and kissed him, delirious with joy. Hugo had made his psychic breakthrough.

Back to the living room. While dancing with her (that dress!), only an ungallant man would not admire what was so visible and alluring. Her breasts were part of her beauty, and she knew it. (To innuendoes as to their possibly artificial nature, she'd reply, "Those who know me better, know better.") And therefore, perhaps foolishly, certainly with more than one drink in me, I remarked, "I should write a poem to them." She nodded quite seriously, sensing the art in the idea. "Yes, you should."

Her eyes demanded honesty and . . . male subservience? Admiration? She suddenly said, "Hey, stop looking at my feet. Look into my eyes. You're hiding again!"

One wanted often to hide one's thoughts.

Another party, a year later, I watched her seated on the windowsill sipping her drink, staring moodily down to the street below. I knew that look more and more. She was floating off in her personal daydream, out of contact, gripped by thoughts that could not be pleasant. I went up to her and said softly, "Hey, psst, come back."

She turned. "I'm going to have sleep trouble again tonight. I get that way now and then." It was the first time she spoke of this. "I'm thinking it's a quick way down from here." I nodded because it was a fact. Silence. She continued. "Who'd know the difference if I went?" I answered, "I would—and all the people in this room who care. They'd hear the crash."

She laughed. Right then and there we made a pact. If either of us was about to jump, or take the gas, or the rope, or pills, he or she would phone the other. We each committed ourselves to talk the other out of it. We made the pact jokingly, but I believed it. I felt that one day I would get a call. She'd say, "It's me, I'm on the ledge," and I'd reply, "You can't jump today, it's Lincoln's Birthday," or something unfunny like that.

It's strange, this premonition that existed between us. I wrote a poem about her some time later in which I envisioned her death with almost prophetic detail. I wanted to show it to her but could not because of the ending. How could I hold up the mirror to her fate that I had somehow divined?

I had written:

> We who spread the rainbow under glass
> And weigh the most elusive sky and air,
> Of that clan I come to track your heart—
> But I'm baffled by those loose strands of hair.
>
> You stand, finger at your lips, lost
> In a long-abandoned heaven. No one within,
> The angels gone, and all the harps undone.
> What legend draws you there? O hurry down!
>
> Surely your home's with us, and not the gods.
> Below your sealed window as you watch,
> A river barge goes by, someone waves,
> You laugh and throw a kiss for him to catch.
>
> You're not to be rescued wholly in this world.
> It must be so. As many who are saved,
> That many drown. I see you clinging
> To rooms, to phones, forgotten to be loved.

She would often hand me a scrap a paper with something written on it and ask, "Do you think this is poetry? Keep it and let me know." Or she'd send a scribbled sheet in the mail asking for criticism. I would always encourage her. The poems were, in the best sense, those of an amateur; that is, they pretended to be nothing more than an outburst of feeling, with little or no knowledge of craft. But the poet within her—and one existed—found a form for her purpose.

As is often the case with poetry, it is a kind of therapy, and what came out of these imperfect scribblings must have surprised her. There are echoes of struggle, search, and torment, with origins we can only guess at.

She wrote:

> Life—
> I am of both your directions
> Existing more with the cold frost
> Strong as a cobweb in the wind
> Hanging downward the most
> Somehow remaining
> those beaded rays have the colors
> I've seen in paintings—ah life
> they have cheated you

The image is repeated on another page written later:

> thinner than a cobweb's thread
> sheerer than any—

but it did attach itself
and held fast in strong winds
and sin[d]ged by (?) leaping hot fires
life—of which at singular times
I am both of your directions—
somehow I remain hanging downward the most
as both of your directions pull me

Hanging downward . . . death? The cobweb . . . umbilical cord: life? Cobwebs are stronger than they appear . . . defiance? These pieces are chaotic attempts to express the darkest contradictory emotions; one senses a desire to hang on to life or plunge into peaceful oblivion (hanging downward). "Both of your directions": life versus death. The great drama was already (always?) within her.

In a totally different vein, she sent me an amusing verse with the inscription "Better if done with a Sir Olivian [Laurence Olivier] accent":

From time to time
I make it rhyme
but don't hold that kind
of thing
against
me—
Oh well what the hell
so it won't sell
what I want to tell—

is what's on my mind
taint Dishes
taint Wishes
its thoughts
flinging by
before I die
and to think
in ink

She was capable of brooding flashes.

Night of the Nite—soothing—
darkness—refreshes—Air
Seems different—Night has
No eyes nor no one—silence—
except to the Night itself

She wrote a lyric fragment entitled "To the Weeping Willow."

I stood beneath your limbs
and you flowered and finally clung to me
and when the wind struck with ... the earth
and sand—you clung to me

There is something especially poignant in the central image. May we not in hindsight interpret the delicate tree clinging to Marilyn in a storm as the storm-tossed Marilyn perhaps clinging to the rooted tree? She would consciously resist the idea that she needed the support; she would be ashamed of the impulse and could express it only through an object. The tree clinging to her gave her the strength of life. Being one with the tree gave her the rootedness she was seeking.

The weeping willow was not merely a symbol; it existed, it had been planted under her watchful eye at her country place. Undoubtedly, she observed the tree from its slender beginnings to a ripening growth. She had this unusual thing about trees. She felt their aliveness. Their leaves were as some miracle; some possible immortality existed in their seasonal dying and rebirth.

The drama of autumn leaves particularly excited her. One late September weekend, I was to join the family in the Connecticut countryside. The hour of departure in the Monroe-Miller household in mid-Manhattan in those days (1957/1958) took on something of a carnival spirit. Here's how I remember it:

The stage is set. The clock is ticking. I am seated in their Manhattan living room with some trepidation. Prospect Park (Brooklyn) is full of lovely leaves, but I am particularly adventurous this Friday. The Connecticut leaf it shall be—and in good company. Food. Fresh air. Fireplace with real fire. Peace. Possibly.

The secretary is hurriedly getting her final letters and appointments checked off, the cook is preparing some food that will supplement country cooking, the phones are ringing. Butch the parakeet is napping in one room, Miller in another.

The doorbell rings. Marilyn enters from shopping, Actors Studio, psychiatrist, either one or all three. Her entrance is always a rush of wind, a flurry of hair. Smiling and mercurial, she greets her visitor (me) with a musical kind of speech.

"I look terrible," she says. (Actually she looks devastating.) "Don't look at me. Turn around. I'm a mess." (It is difficult not to look at her when she enters a room.) "I'm late. Forgive me," she continues. "Give me a minute to wash my face and get into something light." (If she got into anything lighter, she'd blow away.)

I haven't said a word, and now I speak. "You look fine except your eyes are bloodshot, especially the glass one on the right."

She giggles. "My eyes are terrible, I know. I'll have to do something about my eyes." She looks around the room. "Where's Arturo?"

"Asleep, I guess."

"The poor man. He's resting. He works too hard. How about you—can I fix you a drink? Or some milk? There's cake in the kitchen and ice cream."

I blink my eyes, and she's gone. Was it a phone call got her or the secretary or a trap door, or (I think) is she some blithe spirit, a pulsing ghost that comes and goes at her whim?

It's a phone call, or three. I hear her voice.

Enter a man who announces that he's her hairdresser. Short consultation through another door; he leaves, perhaps never to return.

Doorbell. Elevator man says the Jaguar (car) is waiting.

Miller stumbles out of his room, pretending he doesn't know what is going on when in fact he has been hiding under the guise of sleep, which he well knows (knowing the Bard) knits up the raveled sleeve of care. He looks more unraveled than ever.

She returns. He may or may not kiss her, or she may kiss him and he may respond, or he may not. (The romantics who need a security image may imagine them in each other's arms at this moment, oblivious to all, even me, blandly looking on, having nowhere else to look.)

The secretary interrupts with some letters to sign. Marilyn may sign them sitting down, or against the wall, or leaning on Miller's back.

We decide to have one drink before the journey. Marilyn, very energetic, sets up the glasses and pours. "Cheers," she calls out. We drink, she sips.

"We're going to have fun," she says gaily. And then to me, "You'll love the leaves." We chat a while. Miller suggests the bags be brought out to the elevator. Marilyn says she has very little to pack. I have no packing problem: My toothbrush and pound bar of chocolate repose in my pocket. I am, in the deepest sense, committed.

Doorbell. Enter dress designer. Marilyn is reminded that she has an important dinner on Monday night; if she wants her gown ready by then, it has to be fitted right now.

"How long will this take?" inquires Miller, suddenly pale, recoiling a step.

I finger my chocolate bar, very calm.

"It will be half an hour," replies the designer.

"Twenty minutes," commands Miller.

(Silently, I figure one hour.)

Marilyn throws a kiss and skips out. Miller and I say nothing; we are thinking about the lady who just skipped out for a dress fitting and of the chances of getting on the road before dark. I for the leaves, he for the land.

Half an hour goes by. And (miracle!) she appears with her new dress. "How does it look?" she asks, turning seductively.

"Great," I reply.

Miller gives an approving nod. "Yes, very good."

"Five minutes!" she calls out, and vanishes. She has a philosophical insight about time, sensing that it is an arbitrary value, and instinctively disdains the importance put upon it by watchmakers and appointment makers; knowing that time is always beginning and never ending, a symbol of man's helplessness in the face of work to be done.

So that when she says, "Five minutes," she really means, "sooner or later—just relax."

Miller gets the bags out in the hall. In five minutes she appears in slacks, flat shoes, cotton blouse, and scarf around her head. She is surprised at our surprise of her punctuality. It looks like we are on our way. The bags are on the elevator. The last letters are signed. The last hurried phone call. Marilyn carries her drink—champagne—to the elevator. (She loved to drink there, I add this for the amateur psychologist.) The door closes, and we are about to descend when she cries out: "Butch!" Door button pushed, door opens, we all rush back.

On his perch, Butch the parakeet is dreaming of bird seed when Marilyn reaches into the cage and carefully brings him out. "You sweet bird," she croons, "we almost forgot our dear little bird." Butch stands on her open palm, ruffles his wings, and decides to fly around the room. She calls to him (her?), he sits on her shoulder, she coos and whistles, carries him to her lips, and ole Butch leans over and kisses her. Delighted, she lets him fly away. He answers Miller's call, now sits on his hand, gets close to his face but refuses to kiss him. Miller takes this blow to his ego without flinching. Butch tries my shoulder, walks along my outstretched finger and damn near falls off. Finally, into the cage goes Butch, and out to the elevator go all of us. "Oh, you're a cute dar-

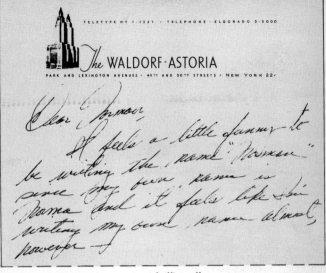

TELETYPE NY 1-1327 · TELEPHONE · ELDORADO 5-3000

The WALDORF-ASTORIA

PARK AND LEXINGTON AVENUES · 49TH AND 50TH STREETS · NEW YORK 22·

Dear Connor,

It feels a little funny to be writing the name "Norman" since my own name is Norma and it feels like I'm writing my own name almost, however —

1955, and all's well.

*Marilyn and author
on the beach.*

"Hey, wait for me!"

*Hedda Rosten and Marilyn —
before the "mini."*

(better if done with an Sir Olivian accent)

for Norman

From time to time
I make it Rhyme
but don't hold that kind
of thing
against
me —

Oh well what the hel
said went sel
what I want to tell —
is whats on my mind   → intended and al to rhyme as tell

taint Dishes
taint Wishes
its thoughts
flinging
before I die I and to think I in ink

Marilyn as weekend sailor.

Marilyn with the Rostens (champagne in trunk compartment).

Marilyn at play.

Marilyn happy,
Olivier glum.

England:
relaxing
after work.

HOTEL DEL CORONADO
Coronado California

September 11, 1958

Dear Norman,

Don't give up the ship while we're sinking. I have
a feeling this boat is never going to dock. We are going
through the Straits of Dire. It's rough and choppy but
why should I worry I have no phallic symbol to lose.

P.S. "Love me for my yellow hair alone"

I would have written this
by hand but its trembling

San Diego — ACROSS THE BAY
Old Mexico — 18 MILES AWAY

A typical Monroe entrance:
with Arthur Miller at Radio City Music Hall.
CULVER PICTURES

Her two worlds,
the private
and the public.

ling," says Marilyn to Butch. Butch loves to hear her voice, figuring she's just as cute a parakeet herself. I believe (and this can be considered a journalistic scoop) that Butch is in love with Marilyn.

The Jaguar is ready. We get in. The bags are in the trunk rack. The brilliant sun is setting over the 59th Street Bridge, a sunset the country people will never know, and we're off!

The details of the two-hour ride will remain forever unrecorded, for I promptly fell asleep in the back seat, securely anchored by my pound bar of chocolate. I don't know what they talked about, but I'm sure it included the wisdom of taking me along, the health of Butch, possibly Miller's health, and whether anyone might break into the house while they were gone. I know it included at least one reprimand by Marilyn that he wasn't paying attention, to which he replied that he certainly was. On the other hand, it may very well have been a trip when Marilyn sulked in the corner of her seat—she could sulk like anyone else. I like to imagine she looked back at least once at my sleeping figure and spoke of the hardship of poets in this commercial age.

We arrive. I stagger out to face the cold moon staring at me over the hill. Marilyn runs to the house shivering with the cold. Miller, the Tolstoian spirit stirring in his bones, pauses only long enough to put the lights on in the house before making a brief tour of his immediate acres. He is very serious about the soil and planting things in the ground. The first half hour in the country always finds him a bit excited, as though he were at last in contact with something permanent. I respect but cannot share his deep breathing and exuberance in the presence of nature. To me, all this is a disguised death wish, and I will have none of it.

The car is unloaded, coffee bubbling, the wood roars in the fireplace. After a short rest, Marilyn checks a feeding station for birds hung from a small maple just outside the door. The birdhouse is half filled with seed, and shreds of suet hang close by.

"Where are all those birds going to feed as they fly south?" she asks. "Especially when we close the house later on, how will they live, poor things."

I remind her that birds manage to get south each year, and come north again. "Yes," she replies, "but so many of them die. It's awful to die when you're helpless, the way a bird is."

While Miller checks through the house (carpenters had been renovating the attic), Marilyn rearranges the living-room furniture. "It's not right this way, it hems me in. I need space. Don't you feel it hems you in?"

About these matters I am most uncertain but help her move a couch and some chairs.

Miller re-enters and stops short. "Are you changing the furniture around again?"

To which she replies, "How do you like it this way?"

He studies the room. "Y'know, it looks pretty good."

She frowns, "No, it's still not right. Something's wrong, but I don't know what. Tomorrow I'll try again." She was never satisfied; she was continually trying to make her home "right" and never succeeded. In the city apartment and the country house, she would change the furniture, remodel the rooms, hang new drapes, etc. The completed home eluded her to the very end.

Later in the evening we sit around the fire and drink coffee and sip cognac. Marilyn talks about a scene she is preparing at the Actors Studio and its difficulties.

"What does Lee think?" asks Miller. He is seated next to her on the couch, relaxed, one arm across her shoulder.

"Lee thinks I can do it." She is deeply affected by Strasberg's faith in her. He is training her, encouraging her, making her believe in herself and in an expanding career. Her gratitude and loyalty never waver. Strasberg is undoubtedly one of the most important influences in her life.

"One thing about Marilyn," exclaims Miller with emphasis. "She can do anything she sets her mind on. She can become a great actress."

Marilyn looks injured. "You mean I'm not there yet?"

He laughs. "You will be, dear. Give it a couple of more weeks."

"He won't write a play for me," she teases. "He's afraid I'll forget my lines. And I could, too!"

"You'd still be a hit. Just by being there, by letting them see you." He nods slowly. Marilyn impulsively reaches over and kisses him.

The next morning I awake to the sound of hammers inside my head. It is not a headache but carpenters at work in the attic or on the roof or under the foundation. Not only are hammers hammering, but saws are sawing. I arise, have a quick breakfast, and flee outside to the peace of nature.

Things are just as bad: birds noisily attacking the barn or one another, a private plane buzzing a cow, somewhere another cow (or bull) bellowing, and across the field a tractor roars. On the tractor is Miller going around in circles but very serious about it, as though this were part of God's plan.

I discover Marilyn seated on the stone fence looking up sadly at several giant elms. They were stripped of leaves and dying.

"It was my fault," she says. "I wanted a stone wall to front the house, and the stone setters went too deep and cut through the big roots. When all the leaves didn't come through that first spring, I knew the trees were hurt. Imagine, those trees were here for over two hundred years, and because of a stone wall that I really didn't need, we killed the trees. Well, almost dead, anyway."

She is genuinely stricken by this accident. They had tried to save the trees, she explains to me. Specialists had pumped vitamins and proteins into the roots, but the trees refused to respond, and hope for them was all but given up. She muses, "It's as though they were punishing us for not appreciating them." I nod, astonished at her giving human motives to a nonhuman object. "But we loved them, I'd never get tired of looking at them. Even in winter, without leaves, they looked beautiful!"

Fortunately, to cheer her up, Hugo came to mind, and with a squeal she runs to the car, calls me to join her, and we're off to get Hugo, who was getting a check-up at the local kennel. One could never tell by looking at him whether or not these sudden reunions pleased him. His face would mask every emotion; like a great actor he kept you guessing. At times—I had seen this reunion often—he would almost smile, but a stiff upper lip got in the way, leaving Hugo with nothing, absolutely nothing.

Hugo loves Marilyn, and she adores him. Beauty and the Beast—Hugo bore out this maxim perfectly. At the kennel, released, he stares at her for a moment, hesitates, comes forward, notices me and takes two steps backwards, stumbles, forward again, almost falls, takes a deep breath, and runs into her arms. She embraces him. "Hugo, how are you? You're beautiful!" (The dog is ugly.) "Good dog, pretty dog, why don't you smile? You're depressed, aren't you?" (He was born depressed. My God, I think, Miller and DiMaggio often have that same look!) "Come, we're going home, and you'll run around and see Arturo and have fun." Hugo nods grimly and enters the car, shrinking from my touch. She talks to him all the way home, and though he doesn't answer, I'm sure he completely understands.

Back at the ranch, we find Miller absorbed in his pet reforestation project: the planting of small pine shrubs on the hillside. The one-foot shrubs are hidden under weeds and wild grass, making them hard to spot. We thereupon, aided by dumb (but lovable) dog, start to hunt for the shrubs to see how they are growing. Before I know it, I'm involved in this game called "Here's one!" Soon I am shouting, "Here's one!" and the three of us (three and a half counting Hugo) are staring down at the small pine shrub. A moment later, Marilyn's voice rings out joyously: "Here's one" and we rush to her side, all staring down again, breathless. She is on her knees, scraping away the dead leaves and grass. The survival of an unprotected shrub on a windy hillside, through rain and frost, is to her a source of trembling joy. She knew her own battle to survive and could appreciate that triumph in nature.

Later that day, speaking about their country retreat, she says, "I suppose everyone needs a place to escape to. With some of us, though, maybe it's all up here." She taps her forehead lightly. "I don't just mean the mind, I mean feeling. It's *feeling* that makes things important." She pauses, then asks abruptly, "Hey, why didn't Hedda come along?"

"It's her lousy cold. Next trip, she promised."

"I miss her. I wish she were here. I've got to make some decisions soon. Should I do my next picture or stay home and try to have a baby again? That's what I want most of all, the baby, I guess, but maybe God is trying to tell me something, I mean with all my pregnancy problems. I'd probably make a kooky mother, I'd love my child to death. I want it, yet I'm scared. Arthur says he wants it, but he's losing his enthusiasm. He thinks I should do the picture." She smiled thinly. "After all, I'm a movie star, right?"

I wrote of her:

Of Gemini born, the twin stars,
Twin demons of her cold sky,
The body aflame, the soul in dread.
Round her the Furies in their black ring

Obscenely mocked, crying *Give us love*.
We watched and bought her anguish with our
coins.

She wrote to my wife and me:

I think I've been pregnant for about three
weeks or may be two. My breast[s] have
been too sore to even touch—I've never had
that in my life before also they ache—also
I've been having cramps and slight staining
since Monday—now the staining is increasing and pain is increasing by the minute.

I did not eat all day yesterday—also last
night I took 4 whole amutal sleeping
pills—which was by actual count really 8 little amutal sleeping pills.

Could I have killed it by taking all the
amutal on an empty stomach? (except I took
some sherry wine also)

What shall I do?
if it is still alive I want to keep it

As it happened Marilyn was not pregnant at
that time. She again turned to her work.

"We must cable Sukarno tonight. Tomorrow
may be too late!" Again, for the third straight
day, Marilyn had brought up the urgency of "res-
cuing" the then president of the Indonesian repub-

lic. The wire services were full of rumors that Sukarno was facing an imminent coup that, if successful, would force him to flee his country. "Are we going to help him or not?" demanded Marilyn. "Where's he going to hide, poor man?"

"That's his problem," countered Miller, at first amused but now annoyed by the subject. "He's not a little boy."

She looked at me appealingly. "Don't you think I'm right?"

I said, "You may be right, but it's not just him—the man has five wives."

"Are you discriminating against him for that?" she flashed back at me.

My wife cut in. "He's sure to have some emergency plans."

"Even so," Marilyn added, "we can at least let him know he has friends in this country."

Miller groaned. We sat in the living room, the news on.

Marilyn said, "We haven't a moment to lose. He could be dead tomorrow, and his wives, too!"

A year earlier, on an official visit to the United States and in the course of a tour of the film studios, Sukarno had requested to meet Marilyn, asserting he was a devoted fan. Marilyn had been thrilled. She recalled that he was handsome and courteous despite the fact that "he kept looking down my dress, you'd think with five wives he'd have enough." She liked him, she liked his fez, she liked his public admittance of his five (or was it four?) wives, all of whom he referred to endearingly. In Marilyn's eyes, that was machismo, romanticism, poetry, and whatever helped explain man's devotion to women. Miller was quick to admit to Sukarno's charm.

"We have got to help him," she went on after a silence.

"Do you want him to move in with those five wives and feed all of them, as well as their children and cats and God knows what else?" Miller was justified in painting this somber picture.

"We have room—if not here, then in the country."

"And if the newspapers pick up your cable, then what? They'll be all over the place asking questions."

She sipped her champagne, sighed, and asked me: "You agree?"

"I think he's right. It's a noble idea, but—"

"Oh shit, you men give me a pain!" She put down her drink and paced the room. "What about friendship? Do you let your friends go down the drain?"

"But dear," said Miller, "he may not want to come here."

"That's why I want to *invite* him here!"

My wife said, "I think your idea is really too impractical, Marilyn. It's a lovely thought, anyway."

She was sullen. "We're letting a sweet man go down the drain. Some country this is."

"It's international politics," said Miller, relieved at her apparent backing down. "He may be out of office this week and in next. Best to forget it."

"You can forget it. I won't."

And she didn't. A week later, with the Indonesian crisis still simmering, she phoned and brought the whole matter up again. "Let's cable him tonight. How about it? In your name if mine's a problem."

"Not in my name, baby. I don't know Sukarno. Even if he gave me one of his wives, I don't think I'd do it. It's just not my problem."

"Coward!" she hissed.

A phone call. 3 A.M. From her maid: "Come quickly!" My wife and I hurry over. Marilyn is in her room, very ill. Her stomach has just been pumped; overdose of pills. It's all quiet; private doctor, no publicity.

My wife enters the room. After a moment I follow into the dim light. I hear someone sobbing quietly. I whisper, leaning over the bed, "It's me, Norman. How are you, dear?"

"Alive. Bad luck." Her voice is rasping, drugged. "Cruel, all of them, all those bastards. Oh Jesus . . ."

She doesn't say who. She has tried this before and will try it again.

Some lines shape in my mind:

> Shadow and light remember her,
> Light of her eyes, grey-green-blue,
> Light dancing in her, from her,
> Woven with the other, the darker, strand.
> Unenduringly alive . . .
>   Sleep
> Entwining her as fern. A dream
> Of unawakening. Sleep she implored,
> Thorn at her heart unrelenting,
> The hopeless gift of love . . .

A note arrived from Coronado, California (September 11, 1958), typed on Hotel del Coronado stationery. The letterhead bore a picture—a print—of the hotel waterfront, to which Marilyn added a tiny figure in the water offshore shouting "help."

Dear Norman,

Don't give up the ship while we're sinking. I have a feeling this boat is *never* going to dock. [She was filming *Some Like It Hot*.] We are going through the Straits of Dire. It's rough and choppy but why should I worry I have no phallic symbol to lose.

                                        Marilyn

PS. "Love me for my yellow hair alone"
[and in a postscript in ink] I would have
written this by hand but it's trembling.

The postscript is a misquoted quote from the
poem "For Anne Gregory" by the great Irish poet
Yeats, a favorite of hers. The actual quote—
which would make hers either ironic or deliberately playful—is as follows:

> ". . . only God, my dear,
>   Could love you for yourself alone
>   And not your yellow hair."

From the Bel-Air in Los Angeles, dated October
27, 1958:

Dear Norman,

Thank you for your Halloween wishes.
It's too bad we can't be together. I might
scare you.

I haven't been writing anyone, let alone
poems—it's so spooky here! Arthur looks
well though weaker—from holding me up.

Whatever happened to the "Mister Johnson Club"? Is Ben still giving free gas? . . . Is
my membership in good standing—because I

need something to hold on to—like a membership card.

e.e. cummings

She was then reading the poetry of e. e. cummings. As for the "Mister Johnson Club," it was impulsively formed by us to commemorate the hero of the novel *Mister Johnson* by Joyce Cary. I had turned that book into a play that was produced on Broadway. In it, the hero, a young African of spirit and imagination who is called Mister Johnson, represented to her the spirit of innocence killed by the "bad guys." Marilyn would say it was "them" against "us" everywhere. The story with its tragic ending left a deep impression upon her. As for Ben and the free gas, he was a gas station owner and friend who was so awed when we once pulled up in her car that he filled her tank without charge; she counted him as the third member of the "Mister Johnson Club." We stopped at three.

"Because I need something to hold on to." That offhand remark in her letter may have hinted at feelings more serious. New strains in Marilyn's life, professional and personal, were beginning to appear. Accompanying her during her film jobs could not have been easy for Miller. He could not have relished the dull routine of movie making, not to mention the atmosphere of the Hollywood community. Marilyn was restless, resentful at her hectic work schedule. The pupil/student had now become a critic. The shadow that had fallen between them in England was increasing, deepening. Their evenings with friends were often played out in a facade of marital harmony. Miller was more and more living with her in the third person, as it were, an observer.

Yves Montand figured briefly though tempestuously in Marilyn's life. A rising film and nightclub star in France in the midfifties—later to become a fine dramatic actor—Montand was teamed with Monroe in the movie called *Let's Make Love*.

Montand and his actress wife Simone Signoret were not unknown to Arthur Miller. They had starred in the French film version of his popular play *The Crucible*. Thus, when Yves came to New York with his successful one-man show in the late fifties, he and Simone met the Millers. We all attended that show together on Broadway. He was a hit. We became friends when I had the courage to point out an awkward moment in his performance. I had noticed that when he would place his hands in his trouser pockets during a song, it slightly spread the trouser flap that covered the buttons of his fly; the buttons glittered in the reflected spotlight. There were titters in the audience, clearly not related to the songs. In his dressing room later, aided by a translator, I told

Yves about this scientific phenomenon. He was astonished. We all laughed, and Yves immediately ordered that a zipper replace the shiny buttons for the next performance. He was very funny describing it, and I liked him.

A late after-theater dinner followed, and then to the Miller apartment for a nightcap. There, relaxing with her favorite champagne, Marilyn and Montand discussed the possibility of costarring in *Let's Make Love*. Yves was worried about his awkward English. Marilyn and Arthur reassured him that it would work out OK. They got along famously.

The deal was made. The filming began. Handsome Yves and sex-symbol Marilyn soon had the gossip mills of Hollywood grinding away. Why did wife Simone Signoret return to Paris during the filming? And didn't husband Arthur Miller spend as much time in New York as he did in Hollywood? Which left the two stars alone. It was known they spent more than the usual time rehearsing their scenes because Yves' English needed additional practice. The titillation of the industry is an old movie with new characters. For a while the underground had a brief torrid affair going, with two marriages headed for the rocks— standard scenario for the colony.

Marilyn personally admired Montand, as well as Simone. She thought Simone—and expressed it often—a remarkable actress. She aspired to that kind of eminence and artistry. Yet one can wonder what the vibrations were between the two women; they could not have been altogether endearing. For it was obvious that Simone's husband was more than enchanted with his costar.

Marilyn referred to Yves as a sensitive and compassionate man. She remarked that he was one who didn't look upon her as only a sex symbol; he was kind and gentlemanly during the making of the film, and thoughtful of women. She hadn't come upon such consideration toward women in all her years in Hollywood. She spoke of him as a funny man and great to work with, avoiding any comment on the rumored romance between them. "He's married," she would say. "I don't get involved with married men."

During the height of the international gossip about them, I was in Paris and decided to pay Simone a visit. I found her address by simply asking a gendarme where she lived; he gave me directions on the spot. Simone was very charming. She remembered our meeting in New York. She had heard the rumors, of course. Like any worldly woman, the possibility of a brief affair did not unduly upset her. What bothered her was the thought that the man she loved would do something foolish and hurt their marriage. She was concerned also about his career. She was, in short, a wife who did not want her husband to suffer any unnecessary consequences, nor did she wish to see Marilyn suffer. A sadness hung over my visit, only partially dispelled by the wine.

The Misfits, directed by John Huston and costarring Clark Gable, was Marilyn's last film. Written by Miller, who also participated in the production, it touched upon a raw nerve, a grinding connection between the fictional and the real life that exhausted her beyond her capacity to recover.

In the film Marilyn portrays a young woman in the process of getting a Reno divorce. Her own divorce loomed ahead; she was, in a sense, rehearsing the role she was shortly to live through. She and Miller were no longer living together; she knew they would separate at the end of the picture. He was her writer-producer. Once he was her hero—the artist above the show-biz jungle—teacher, lover, protector, father, and man of integrity to shield her against the world's assaults, real or imagined. Yet what man could fulfill this role, answer her desperate needs and consuming demands? She had given him all she was able to give, whatever love she had. Now it was over. The "hero" had become the "enemy"—a representative of the movie industry, using her much the same way as the others. The husband/protector was no longer there; they were now involved in a business arrangement.

Months before the actual shooting, she struggled against interpretations in the script. She felt the heroine was too passive. In a three-way telephone conversation between her Connecticut home and my summer rental a hundred miles away, she, Miller, and I talked about his screenplay. It wasn't my idea at all. She had mailed me the script a week earlier and now asked over the phone, "What'd you think of it?" I said I thought it would make a good film. Miller grunted on the extension. She asked me to turn to a crucial speech that she pronounced as "lousy." Miller grunted again, or possibly it was a growl. "The speech is too goddam long," she said, "and anyway, it isn't right." She paused, waiting for me to say something. I preferred not to. The privacy of the writer was no academic point to me. I had gone through this scene many times, listened to actors, agents, and producers telling me to change this, rewrite that. And so I sympathized fully with Miller here. She was the star. He was the writer. She could suggest changes, not demand them. And certainly not make them publicly.

Well (she seemed to imply), if he is the producer, she's going to fight for her rights as the actress. And she did. With the gloves off. Was she fighting him for script changes or putting the screws into him as a parting shot in a fading marriage? "I want this speech rewritten," she said harshly into the phone. "Are you there, Arthur?"

His voice, controlled, at the edge of anger, "I'm here."

"Well, what are you going to do about it?"

"I'm going to think about it."

"Norman agrees with me."

I cut in. "I didn't agree, Marilyn. I agreed to read the screenplay, which I did. If Arthur asks my opinion on certain scenes or speeches, I'll tell him." She was silent, I could hear her frustrated breathing. Always the gentleman and coward, I said, "Look, it's a draft, I'm sure there'll be more work on it. I mean, it's not final, is it?"

Miller responded listlessly. "It's a draft."

Peacemaker and idiot that I was, I continued, "Maybe that section can be trimmed. If Marilyn has specific objections—!"

"I object to the whole stupid speech," she said. "And he's going to rewrite it!"

She was giving him the business, making him eat the Hollywood shit even as they made her eat it for so long. She was fighting the pain and humiliation of another rejection, of one more failure in love. She was aware this was to be their last shared experience. She knew, too, that Miller wanted the film made even if it meant continuing the fiction of their marriage. Yes, she could be vengeful. For she was alone now, exhausted after *Let's Make Love,* which had been completed a few weeks earlier. She was in no physical or emotional state to begin another film, particularly of this nature. She was alone, the old fears rising. She was threatened, and she struck back. Her claws were showing; they had a right to show. She was fighting for her life.

And for Miller as well, the loss of what—for all the contradictions—had surely begun as love. His disillusion, his bursts of tenderness, show in the film. They reveal his real attitude toward the marriage. And Marilyn did not flinch in her performance.

The shooting was another tightrope affair, a day-to-day peril. At one point Marilyn, her speech blurred, could no longer proceed. It looked like the end. Director Huston was desperate. He phoned Marilyn's analyst in Los Angeles, who arranged to admit her into a small private hospital as a medical patient in the care of an internist, and together they managed to get her off all barbiturates. At the end of ten days she was able to return to work, taking no medication during the day and only the mildest sleeping medication at night. But no one could really relax. Too much was going on within her. Each day was a mountain to climb, a river to cross.

Her first shot in the *The Misfits*: She's seated before a mirror painting on lipstick. A face of unearthly sadness and purity. I think of the poet Rilke's lines: "For Beauty's nothing/ but beginning of Terror we're still just able to bear . . ." At her mirror, she is rehearsing a visit to the divorce court, repeating the "cruelty" charge to make sure she's phrasing it correctly for the judge. She is numb, afloat, at the edge of terror.

In a following scene with her husband (Kevin McCarthy), she rejects his overture for reconciliation, summing up their relationship with: "You aren't there." (It was her favorite expression in recounting experiences with men: They were rarely "there.")

In a scene set in the desert house with her new acquaintances, Gay and Guido (Clark Gable and Eli Wallach), Roslyn (Marilyn) discusses marriage and divorce. She is given the line: "Husbands and wives are killing each other." It is a line written by Miller and delivered by her with an intensity that vibrated throughout the film, as though a confessional understood by both.

Marilyn's euphoric moment of walking up and down the single step leading into the unfinished house is beguiling. The house, the joy of being loved, the path so often taken and here taken again with freshness and hope, reveal a transcendent spirit that Miller recognized.

At one point, Gay says to Roslyn, "I'd marry you." They are in love now; he is an aloof man, and his decision is bewildering even to himself, but he wants to commit himself here and now. She replies, "It's nice of you to say it, but you don't have to." She is quite willing to be his mistress, that would be satisfying enough. She doesn't expect more. Or is it that she feels she doesn't deserve more, is unworthy of more? To me, it reveals the woman willing to risk all on being loved, the man reassuring her of his honorable intentions. The moral man versus the creature of feeling.

There is another crucial scene to consider, the sharpest mirror of her anguish, life rerun as art. Roslyn, talking with Gay after an attempt to resolve their differences, says, "Love me." Alone for a moment, immediately after, she utters a single muted word: "Help!" "Love me"—"help." The desperate cry—it was her lifetime cry—followed by the word that may be the key to the puzzle. Is she asking for help, or is it a cry of inadequacy? As if to say: "Help me to bear being loved, and not kill what I love."

Or, could not her cry have sprung from another yet deeper source of her torment? In the scene before, cowboy Perce, Gay, Guido, and Roslyn are returning to Guido's home after a wild day at the rodeo where Perce had been injured. They are all exhausted. Guido is driving, Roslyn sits with one arm around the sleeping Perce, the other around Gay, also asleep at her breast. Guido, driving crazily, is saying to Roslyn, "The difference is that I *see* you. You're the first one I ever *saw* . . . Help me. I never said help before in my life . . . At least say hello Guido." He asks dumbly for her to recognize him, save him.

Once in the house she covers the hurt Perce with a blanket. He mumbles, "No, Ma, don't, don't!" She answers a neurotic mother need for him. Finally, alone with Gay, he asks her if she'd ever want a child with him. He wants a chance to make up for the mistakes he made with his now grown children; he needs her for this atonement. Roslyn is unable to answer him. Gay is irritated by the presence of the other two men. Roslyn, sensing his doubt and suspicion, asks of Gay only, "Oh, love me, Gay!" It is then that she cries to the night sky: "Help!"

There is a pattern here of male dependence. Each man looks upon her as the one who can change his life and make him whole. Each wants her love, her concern. She is being torn apart by the needs of others. None of these strong men— not even Gay, her lover—seems to care much what *she* wants or needs. And her needs are more desperate than theirs.

At one searing moment near the end of the film, when the men are brutally tying up the last of the wild horses destined for dog meat, Roslyn turns to them—it's a scene out of control—and screams: "You are the killers!" At this moment, the men may have looked upon her as the crazy misfit, but in her eyes they were the true outcasts, without values, rootless. She, at least, was fighting for something.

The Misfits is the one work that may tell more

about the Miller-Monroe story than most analytic conjectures. That Marilyn was able to wear a fictional mask during this period was surely an act of courage, a triumph of will and professionalism. She must have been aware, also, of the presence on the set of photographer Inge Morath, covering the film for Magnum. She could not but help sense something between her husband and the woman who would in the near future become his third wife. But she had agreed to do this job, and she wasn't copping out.

The Misfits completed, Marilyn returned to New York. November 1960. She and Miller each made a formal announcement of their separation and pending divorce. It was the beginning of a black winter for her. A week or so after her return East her friend and costar Clark Gable died of a heart attack. Gable was her fantasy father, she never saw her real father. She remembered that her mother (before commitment) had kept a photograph of Clark Gable on the bureau; she grew up with this powerful identification. She had a close friendship with him through many critical weeks of the film. His kindness and consideration sustained her. ("The place was full of so-called men, but Clark was the one who brought a chair for me between the takes," she told me.) His death came as a blow. And Marilyn's tentative hold on herself weakened. She fell into a depression. During this period, without fanfare, she went to Mexico where her marriage was legally terminated.

Back to her New York apartment, she spent days alone in her darkened bedroom. She refused to see any of her old friends: only the Strasbergs had access to her. Most calls were not put through, and on a few occasions when my wife did reach her on the phone her voice was blurred, distant, unhappy.

Some weeks after the divorce, she phoned. "Hey, how's everybody?" It was her old voice with the lilt gone.

"We're all fine here, Marilyn," I replied.

"I know you're friends with the other guy, but I hope we can be friends, too."

"We can, dear. We will be, I promise you that."

"I'm glad." There was a pause.

I asked, "Where are you now?"

"In my apartment, just back from Mexico."

"Would you have dinner with us tonight?"

"You'd better ask Hedda, maybe."

"I'm asking you. For both of us."

"OK. I'll be there."

She said to me later, "I went to the country house one day last week with a small truck and a driver to pick up a few odd pieces of iron porch furniture. They were old sentimental pieces, not worth much, but they always followed me wherever I went, and I wanted them again. Maybe worth fifty dollars. Sort of good luck, I mean hard-luck, pieces. So I called my ex about it, and he said sure come up any time and take them, if I'm not here you know where the key is. I told him when I'd be there, but when I got there he wasn't. It was sad. I thought he'd be there and maybe ask me in for coffee or something. We spent some happy years in that house. But he was away. And then I thought, Maybe he's right, what's over is over, why torment yourself with hellos? Still, it would have been polite, sort of, don't you think, if he'd been there to greet me? Even a little smile would do."

Marilyn had a special relationship with Arthur Miller's father, Isidore. He was more than a father-in-law; he stirred within her the affection toward a real father. She was touched by his tenderness and concern. A man of little if any formal education, an immigrant, Mr. Miller had the instinctual reflexes of a gentleman. He enjoyed teasing Marilyn, and she was a perfect buff for his deadpan gags. Yes, she truly adored him; he was the big gruffy gentle bear, the father who would never hurt her.

The divorce left him heartbroken. They continued to phone one another and occasionally meet for lunch. She worried about his health, he about her future; she would visit him when she learned he was ill.

The old fears again. And again, the pills to help her sleep. Her manner was evasive, she would not return calls. She was more depressed than I had ever known her.

Finally, her doctor decided that Marilyn needed hospitalization. By this time her dependence on drugs indicated that something drastic had to be done. She was persuaded to enter the Payne-Whitney Clinic in New York without being told it was a mental hospital. When she found out, she was shocked, frightened, and felt betrayed.

A young crew-cut doctor, fresh out of medical school, tried to calm her. Instead of answering her questions, he repeatedly kept asking, "Why are you so unhappy?" Enraged, she answered, "I've been paying the best doctors a fortune to find out why, and you're asking *me*?" At one point (for reasons I've never been told) she threw a chair through a glass door. They put her in a guarded room and took away her clothes. Here she was, distraught, alone, her career and life in shambles, detained in an institution—exactly as her mother! The irony and terror must have been indescribable. Now she called upon one person she knew she could depend on, Joe DiMaggio—Joe the Slugger as she often referred to him—and he came to her rescue. According to Marilyn, he threatened to take the hospital apart brick by brick if she was not released at once. He signed the papers, and she was out. With great pleasure and pride she recounted that scene. "That's the kind of ballplayer Joe is!"

From there it was a short trip across town to Columbia Presbyterian Hospital where she was willing to accept further treatment and care. During one of our visits, my wife and I found her lying pale and distracted on the upraised bed, a nurse sponging her damp forehead. She lifted her hand weakly and smiled; her energies seemed at a new low. She was ill, not only of the body and mind, but of the soul, the innermost engine of desire. That light was missing from her eyes.

3.

*". . . Fame will go by and, so long,
I've had you, fame."*

California. 1962. Her last spring. She had then only a few more months of life.

To start again after a third marital failure would demand a colossal effort and control. She was back in Hollywood, the circle closing. Not a return in triumph but in default; she was back because she had nowhere else to go. One always goes home when the world cannot be won. She had moved to her new house—the small, never-to-be-completed house that she wanted so desperately to make into a permanent home. It was built in Mexican style: tiles, masks on the wall, assorted pottery, and a large Aztec calendar decorated the rooms. But they were cold, uncertain, incomplete rooms. White sheets covered the bedroom windows. Not much furniture, as though she were unsure of the house and its occupant. In the back, a small swimming pool, some lawn, and a few trees on perhaps an acre of land that fell away in a deep cut, affording a modest view. Far from the Beverly Hills splendor, but she liked the setting.

Alone again, she was feverishly optimistic. Yes,

she looked forward to work, a new film, a resumption of her career. Did she hear the rumors that she was through? If so, she never referred to them. She talked about the future. Fate was now watching her, knowing just how much time was left, stepping around the garden, getting accustomed to the grounds, peering into the window of her bedroom where her lifeless body would soon be discovered. And I, listening to her, aware only of a controlled desperation. Ruth amid the alien corn. The land of the drive-in.

Several days after our arrival (my wife and I were in Hollywood on a film assignment), Marilyn phoned and excitedly announced, "It's Sunday, let's go to my analyst. I want you and Hedda to meet him. I told him and his wife that we're coming."

I hesitated. "Is that allowed?" (I never had an analyst.)

"He's a great person and has a wonderful family," she said, leaving my question unanswered. "You'll like them all and vice versa."

"What'll we do—talk about you?"

"It's OK. As long as I'm not listening. Phone you right back."

In a few minutes she reported that we were not only invited to his house but could stay on and listen to chamber music; we learned that her analyst played violin with an amateur quartet. "Chamber music!" she gayly exclaimed. "And it's not in a chamber, it's in a living room!" She was happy at the prospect of enjoying *chamber* music, elite music, the champagne of music.

Introductions at her analyst took on a touch of elegance, if that's the right word. I was not just a writer but her "poet friend," while Hedda was not only my wife but "a dear person, and they're happily married."

Our host, Dr. Ralph Greenson, and his family were gracious and wonderfully informal. Marilyn fitted in easily. One could sense her complete relaxation here, as though this were a second home (a warmer foster home, the thought flashed through my mind). The house was in Mexican style, and I realized that Marilyn was modeling her own house after this one. It was, in fact, a miniature, a replica of this one. "I am trying to grow up, Doctor," her actions seemed to be saying. "I think I can now move away, but I want some reminders of home." In a way, her attempt to build a replica of her doctor's home was a touching sign of affection as well as an indication of beginning independence.

Finally, after coffee and cake and idle Sunday chatter, the other musicians showed up. Soon a familiar Mozart string quartet danced upon the air. Marilyn's analyst, it can be mentioned, played with the passion of the dedicated amateur, and what was lost in a few dropped notes he more than made up for in energy and tone. All in all, a perfect afternoon.

We returned on several other occasions, enjoying these interludes in an otherwise dull work routine. Sometimes I'd bring a friend for the talk and good music. I recall Marilyn and screenwriter Ira Wallach in the kitchen having a heated argument. He contended that all wars were, in hindsight, pointless and absurd. Marilyn challenging, "What about Hitler?" Ira retorted, "Winning World War II hasn't changed history very much." Marilyn was stern. "Ira, you're the most sardonic man I've met. You don't believe in anything!"

Later, when I questioned Dr. Greenson about how Marilyn was progressing, he said, "It may seem odd to you the method I am using to treat her, but I firmly believe that the treatment has to suit the patient and not vice versa. Marilyn is not an analytic patient, she needs psychotherapy, both supportive and analytical. I have permitted her to become friendly with my family and to visit in my home because I felt she needed actual experiences in her present life to make up for the emotional deprivation she had suffered from childhood onward. It may seem to you that I have broken rules, but I feel that if I am fortunate enough, perhaps some years from now, Marilyn may become a psychoanalytic patient. She is not ready for it now. I feel I can tell you these things because she considers you and Hedda her closest friends and there must be somebody with whom I can share some of my responsibilities. By the way, I have spoken to Marilyn and she has given me permission to talk to you in general terms about herself."

At another time, Dr. Greenson related an incident which revealed a little-known aspect of her character. "We decided to give our daughter Joanie a birthday party. Surprise for our guests: Marilyn was invited and she came! After an initial shock, several boys took turns dancing with her, and soon all of them were on line. It didn't look too promising for the local girls. And no one was dancing any more with an especially attractive black girl who, until Marilyn arrived, had been the most popular on the floor. Marilyn noticed this, and went over to her. 'You know,' she said, 'you do a step I'd love to do, but don't think I know how. Would you teach it to me?' Then she turned to the others and called out, 'Everybody stop for a few minutes! I'm going to learn a new step.' Now, the point is, Marilyn knew the step, but she let this girl teach it to her. She understood the loneliness of others."

We met often during this period and talked about old times and laughed at things that went wrong in her life. She seemed to be able to talk about the past easily. It was a happy time for all of us.

Marilyn, Hedda, and I were at a Hollywood restaurant one evening, a quiet farewell dinner for my wife's departure the next morning; she was returning home to our daughter while I planned to stay on for a week or two longer. Playwright William Inge was free that night (he was a friend accidentally discovered in our motel), and he came along. Marilyn had starred in his film, *Bus Stop,* which became one of her biggest triumphs.

She remarked how wonderful it was that Hedda trusted me to remain here alone. "You don't know this town," she said. "It's full of husbands on the prowl."

"I never prowl," I grinned evilly. "I just sit still and howl."

"I'm not worried. He needs me to correct his grammar." Hedda turned to Marilyn. "I'll miss you. Please take care of yourself. Promise you'll rest up before the really hard work begins on the film."

Marilyn nodded. "I'm in good shape, honest. Well, in body if not in mind." She laughed and tapped her forehead. "It's all up here, you know. Or so they say." She waved to someone across the room. A lean, handsome, slightly graying man rose from his table and started toward us. It was Joe DiMaggio.

Inge recognized him, and it seemed to me as if he paled a bit and shrank down in his chair. The idea that Big Joe might consider him Marilyn's escort apparently shook him. But DiMaggio was completely charming as he came up. He smiled, reached over for her hand and pressed it between his own. In a low but not unmusical voice he asked, "How are you, Marilyn?"

She answered, "Fine, Joe." She turned, introducing him. "This is Joe DiMaggio. You know, one of my ex's."

"Right," said Joe amiably. He dropped her hand and stood erect.

She then introduced us with a kind of comic formality. "These are my friends from New York, Norman and Hedda Rosten. And this is a writer, Bill Inge."

Bill said, "Nice to meet you, Mr. DiMaggio."

Joe grinned and said to Marilyn, "Didn't you just leave a writer?"

"I never knew there were so many of them," she replied. We laughed.

All shook hands across the table. "Everything going OK?" he asked her. "The new picture shaping up?"

"Right, Joe. I'm hoping it works out."

He put his fist playfully against her jaw. "It will, honey. You have what it takes." He nodded to us and walked away.

"Joe the Slugger," she said. "Now that I'm back, he keeps an eye on me, sort of. If I have any trouble, I just call on Joe. It makes me feel safe. We didn't make it together, who knows why? When I married him, I wasn't sure of *why* I married him. I thought I was sure with the next one, but it didn't turn out, either. They all had good points," she added with a wan smile.

One late afternoon, I received a call from her. As usual, she got right to the point. "Can you come over? I'm going out to dinner, and I want you to meet my date. Can't tell you who it is on the phone. We'll have a drink first. Bye!" I didn't know why she couldn't tell me over the phone— as though anything could be kept secret in Hollywood.

I dropped by. She stuck her head out of a side room as I entered, her hair in curlers, makeup half on, and called, "I'll be a few minutes! Go on into the back room. I told him about you. You'll recognize him."

He was Frank Sinatra. He rose to greet me, extending his hand. "Hello, Marilyn said you'd come by. She said I had to meet you. Or else." His manner was casual and friendly yet surprisingly serious. We sat while the maid brought me a drink. We asked the routine questions of the trade. He spoke about his recent trip to Europe and went into some detail of a stopover in Germany. He wasn't sure about the Germans. After about fifteen minutes of talk, he looked at his watch. We caught each other's smile. He said, "She's a good kid, but not always on time."

I spoke about my work in Hollywood, which didn't interest him much, though he listened politely. We talked about writers and films, but it was killing time, and we knew it. When was the lady going to appear? We were getting on to the hour mark and still no Marilyn. Frank was plainly showing his annoyance. Marilyn's lateness had always annoyed people, but they put up with it. Reasons are many and fruitless. She is late because of some inner fear. She is late because it's her way of testing your patience and love. She's late because she can't tell time. She's late because she's just plain bitchy. I've heard the most elaborate examinations of Marilyn's inability to be on time. And Marilyn's answer is: "Gee, I don't mean to be late. I'm sorry." Anyone brave enough to challenge that explanation is a fool.

I recalled her analyst, in response to my query about her lateness, saying: "People always speak of her coming late. On her first few appointments with me, she did indeed come late. I said to her, 'Do you know what it means to me when you come late? It means: I don't like you, Doctor Greenson. I don't want to come and see you.' Her reply was childish, surprised, 'Oh no, I do like to come and see you. I do.' I'd answer, 'Your words say that. Your actions say: I don't like you, Doctor.' Well, she never came late again. She'd often eat her lunch seated in her car in the driveway not to come late. And not only did she not come late, she started to show up early. Too early. Half an hour, then one whole hour early. So you see," he smiled, "she was still charmingly mixed up about time."

Maybe she came early for her analyst, but at this moment she is definitely late, and Mr. Sinatra must bide his time, which he does as do all sensible men.

Then she appears, and it's a shock. Marilyn is dressed in a pale-green print dress of simple design. It is modestly cut at the neck and flared at the bottom. Her shoes are pale green, her stockings flesh-colored. She is wearing a green tinted ribbon in a bow at the back of her hair and earrings of another time and place. The shock, of course, is the realization that she is dressed like a young girl, on her way possibly to a school dance. She is back to age sixteen or eighteen. She appears high-spirited, giddy, a bit nervous (girl on first date?). Sinatra is on his feet now, anxious to leave. Marilyn makes a point to tell Frank that I'm a poet, and he dutifully nods. "If you need a good writer for a movie, he's great," she says, squeezing my arm. Frank and I now nod together. Then she thanks me for coming by. We go out the door together. They get into his car, and she turns and waves as though she hasn't a care in the world.

The next morning, I am awakened at 7:30

A.M. by the phone. "What'd you think?" Her voice is eager.

"Think of what?" I suddenly hate this nonsense.

"Of him. Frankie."

"What about him?"

"Did you like him?"

"I thought he was OK. He's an attractive man."

"He's nice, isn't he?" She sounded excited. "I thought you'd like him."

What was this all about? It did seem almost like a girl on her first date. After all, she knew Sinatra from back in the old Hollywood days. Why this sudden intensity? Was she serious about him? I was new to the scene, this added another confusion in my mind. Later, I thought the tone in her voice was not eagerness but panic.

Sometime earlier I had sent her a half-hour tape of a poetry reading I gave over a local station. It was my birthday present to her. I knew she'd enjoy the poems, but more than that she would know I still considered her a good listener of poetry and that I thought of her. She was alone now, facing a difficult adjustment; those poems I sensed would help, they were my proxy.

When I came out to Hollywood shortly after, I was told by her secretary that she carried my tape everywhere with her in her handbag as a sort of good-luck charm. She also bought a new machine to play the tape. On the particular evening she wanted me to hear it, I was also scheduled to attend a screening of a film related to my present assignment. Marilyn, discussing this on the phone, said that was fine: I would come early, her maid would prepare coffee, and we'd listen together; she would listen in bed and would go to sleep right after the tape ended; she wouldn't even have to get out of bed since the machine had an automatic shutoff. That is, she quickly added, if I should decide to leave before the tape ended.

I arrive. She's in her pajamas. Coffee is ready. We drink and talk. Her work and plans. My work and plans. My wife and daughter. My work here and how soon I'll be leaving. She hopes her new film will really move ahead; she's nervous but ready. She gets into bed; I sit on the floor nearby next to the machine. She says, "I took a little pill before you came, so I may be going right off while hearing your voice. OK?"

"And I may sneak out before it's over."

"I try to get to sleep early these days, but if you feel like using the house some evening, please come by. There's a small back door behind the hedge that I'll leave open. Come in any time, stay as long as you like, use the records. I have Bach and Vivaldi, also lots of singers. And there's champagne on ice. You'll be no bother at all. Please, we're friends."

I nod. My voice begins on the tape:

Things used to happen to me more often.
Such as, I'd be sitting in a park
And a hunchback would ask me for a light.
Or a mother would say, Please watch my baby,
As she climbed a tree to eat a blossom.
More than once I'd hold one end
Of a jumping rope for children.
I'd always be asked directions by foreigners,
Not to mention an occasional prostitute
Pretending to be lost: how did she know
I was as well?

A quick laugh. She says, "Great."

        I've been mistaken
For a Greek, a lawyer, a smiling fool,
Even Will Rogers—

"Claude Rains!" she blurts out.

        —and the point is
I'm not only not any of them
But shaky as to what I really am.

Being reflected in the eye of others
Has a certain tenderness: we survive
On the mercy of madmen and strangers.
We should be out on the streets more often,
Where mistakes happen, and lives are saved.

She listens, her eyes closed, the lines around her mouth relaxed. Her eyes open, warm and languid, and close again. As the next poem is being read, her head drops slightly; she listens and reacts, her eyes open again, observing me, sending out a smile. I smile back faintly. I want more than ever a possible happiness for her and feel powerless to help her.

About fifteen minutes pass, the silence broken only by my voice on the tape. She raises her hand and whispers. "You can leave if you have to, I'll listen by myself. It's beautiful. Thanks for sending it."

I passed the bed, stopped and squeezed her hand lying on the coverlet. She was close to sleep. I went out the door, tired of my own voice following me, tired suddenly of an obligation I wished were not mine.

She seemed to be obsessively concerned with my health and welfare away from home. Once, coming to pick me up at my motel, she discovered me chatting with an attractive girl at the switchboard. She brought up the subject later. "I want you to stay away from that girl," she said. "You're happily married." I glowered in my Humphrey Bogart manner: "So? What about it?" She said, "So don't go flirting with these chicks. I'll call your wife." She was serious. She had this protectiveness toward women she liked. She said she intended keeping tabs on me. I told her any marriage that couldn't weather some outside flirting wasn't very solid. She shook her head. "You cut it out, that's all!" She could be very unfair.

Nevertheless, I understood her motive—a groping toward some definition of love, that mystery never explained clearly to herself, the labyrinth from which she never escaped. At the age of thirty-five, she had found the world full of deception and betrayal; her overromantic reaction was to picture me as a model husband without a single extramarital thought. She hated the idea of people sleeping around; love, to her mind, made that an act of hypocrisy. She had obviously not done too well herself in her love life; instinct had failed her, and her new rational approach was not going to unlock any great secret. Intelligence has never been the key to anyone's psychic discovery; one arrives by a chain of feeling, in her case so dense and entangled as to perhaps make a discovery impossible altogether. It was the cruelest irony: the love goddess starving for lack of it.

During this last spring of her life, was she any closer to discovery and fulfillment? She was courageous but not superhuman. The new house was a beginning, it represented a possible security. Yet, it meant coming back home, and home is where the ghosts are always waiting. The Industry giveth and the Industry taketh away. Hollywood, the dream factory, had created a dream girl. Could she awake into reality? And what was that reality? Was there a life for her outside of the dream? Marriage and motherhood—that crucial reality had faded away: Was there any other for her? It seemed improbable that a new life could be found in the land of the scorpions.

The day for my departure East arrived, and I had come to say good-by. It was the last time I would see her alive. It was noon. Her maid woke her, and she stumbled out into the living room buttoning her robe: face heavy-lidded, bloated, drugged with sleep. The love goddess wasn't looking too good. She moved to the window, shading her eyes. "God, it's going to be a real dull Sunday."

I said, "I see you got the pool lit up."

She said, "You're going home, aren't you? Have a nice trip and say hello to all."

It was that kind of bad disconnected talk. After six weeks in California, my leaving clearly frightened her. She wanted people near her, to be *there*. She always needed someone, to listen, to smile or laugh, to argue, to create a human environment; alone, the void opened up before her, endless and terrifying.

I suggested, to cheer her spirits, we drive into Beverly Hills and check some of the art galleries that might be open. She agreed; in fact, it seemed to snap her awake. She decided to change, and after a while she came out of her room dressed in slacks, a shirt, a bandanna over her head. And those wild sunglasses, her "disguise" that invariably succeeded only in drawing attention to her. (Hide and seek. Who am I?)

The chauffeur-driven Cadillac moved down the hot road. She brought along a picnic lunch, cold steak sandwiches and coffee, and we ate in silence. She was brooding, distracted. She said, "You never swam in the pool, you're a lousy friend." I nodded. I wasn't a very good friend; I knew she wanted to show off her pool. But I had been busy, and here it was my last day, and I had never tested the water. "On my next visit, I promise," I said, very seriously, for it seemed to mean so much to her.

Well, I thought, here I am, seven years later, being her escort again. But it was a different world. A sadder time. And overhead, the bright fairy-tale sun of Sunland. We found a gallery that featured an exhibition of modern paintings. Marilyn began to relax and enjoy herself. She bought a small oil by Poucette, a red abstract study. Then her eye caught something not in the regular exhibit: a Rodin statue—a bronze copy, one of twelve—no more than two feet high. It depicted the full figures of a man and woman in an impassioned embrace: a lyric, soaring image. The man's posture was fierce, predatory, almost brutal; the woman innocent, responding, human. Marilyn looked at the statue for a full minute, then decided to buy it. The price was over one thousand dollars. I suggested she think about it. No, she said, if a person thinks too long about something, it means he doesn't really want it. She wrote out a check.

We drove back with the statue. She held it balanced on her lap and stared at it. Shaking her head, she marveled aloud. "Look at them both. How beautiful. He's hurting her, but he wants to love her, too." It seemed to confirm some deep feeling of exhilaration and fear. Then I recalled how, years earlier in New York, we had spent an hour in the Rodin section at the Metropolitan Museum of Art. She had been enraptured with the exquisite white marble figures of "The Hand of God." The lovers entwined in that Hand represented then an ecstacy she could dream of and possibly achieve. Now the miracle was behind her, unrealized.

For some unexplainable reason, her mood shifted from cheerful to sullen, possibly even hostile. She said abruptly, "We'll stop off at my analyst. I want to show him the statue."

"Now?" I asked. I was worried about this turn of events.

"Sure," she mumbled. "Why not now?"

I said it was wrong to go unannounced. Whereupon Marilyn stopped at her house, phoned him while I waited in the car, and triumphantly returned with the news that we had permission to drop by. She leaned forward inside the car and called out with a giggle, "On to my doctor!"

He greeted us courteously. Marilyn immediately set the statue on the sideboard adjoining the bar, announcing her purchase with pride. "What do you think?" she asked stridently, turning toward him. He replied quietly that it was a striking piece of art. Marilyn seemed unusually restless and kept touching the bronze figures. A belligerence crept into her speech. "What about it? What does it mean? Is he screwing her, or is it a fake? I'd like to know. What's this? It looks like a penis." She was referring to what appeared to be a bronze spur attached to the casting. It seemed to pierce the woman's body. After a sober examination we decided it wasn't a penis. Marilyn kept repeating, her voice shrill, "What do you think, Doctor? What does it mean?"

A hidden drama was exploding. She was demanding something, a desperate question, the heart's innermost mystery—a question impossible for any mortal to answer. The tenderness of love, the brutality, the meaning if it existed, what was it, how to feel, recognize, be protected against? Everything inscrutable was in her question. The truth was—it struck me with a sudden force—she was falling apart. This was the moment of her total bewilderment. Had she come home for the debacle, the ultimate letting go? Was Hollywood,

the most unreal city, to be the fated crypt of her
unreal daughter?

From the dark where we created her,
Big Screen America, Vista Land, Color Land,
Dream Land, Whore Land ...
We gave her a name and a terror,
Projected her with a monster's eye ...

We drove back to her house shortly after. We
had some chilled champagne. She seemed a bit
more cheerful. The statue found a place on the
living-room table, she placed it there carefully
and stepped back to admire it. I mentioned the
time; my plane was leaving in a few hours. She
said she'd have a poolside party on my next visit,
just for me. I swore I'd stay in the pool then until
they fished me out.

I rose. "I hope the new film goes well, Marilyn."

"We did some test scenes of me in a pool, sort
of nude. I hope they give me some good nude
lines to go with it." She laughed, but it was a
weary laugh.

A final sip of champagne, a light embrace, and
I got into my car. She said, "Give everybody a
kiss at home." I turned to wave as my car started
to move toward the gate. She stood at the door-
way and waved back, her face pale and unbear-
ably poignant, that face known in every corner

of the world and now fading from my sight forever.

She never did get very far into the new film—her last—with its cruelly ironic title: *Something's Got To Give.* She had been scheduled to begin work for 20th Century-Fox in February, but it wasn't until April that Marilyn reported to the studio. We would get calls from her when we returned to New York. She still wasn't happy about the script; she was, however, glad to be working again, relieved to dispose of her final obligation to the Fox studio. But her old problems pursued her. There followed delays, minor illnesses, strange absences: collision ahead.

One day she phoned. A flash of the old breathless Monroe: "Hello, hello, notice my voice is low because I'm coming East on sort of a secret mission, well it won't be secret after I'm there. I'm going to sing for the president at a birthday party in New York. I won't be able to see you, I'll have to fly right back and get to work." Almost her old laugh. "The press will get a big surprise about my escort. Who do you think is taking me to the party? My ex father-in-law, no kidding, Isidore Miller! He agreed. Isn't he a darling?"

Marilyn created a sensation by appearing at Madison Square Garden to sing "Happy Birthday" for President John Kennedy during a political rally in the spring (May 21) of 1962. She wore a close-fitting flesh-colored dress adorned with cut-glass stones, a daring creation, and delivered the song in a way it has never been delivered before or since. A low, husky, throbbing, fantastic voice, not of a singer but of a woman who had grown and suffered and was reaching down into a final source of strength. It was the year of her death, and the man for whom she sang would himself be assassinated not many months after her own suicide.

Was there a final phone call to a member of the Kennedy family on the night of her suicide? The rumors were never substantiated.

Attempts to link Robert Kennedy and Marilyn often arose out of absurd conjecture and gossip. For example, at a dinner party given in Santa Monica by Peter Lawford, his brother-in-law at that time, the visiting Mr. Kennedy was seated between Monroe and Kim Novak. Drama: which of these lovely women would most intrigue our political hero? It seemed to the observing guests that Marilyn got his attention early, and held it throughout the dinner. Romantic overtones were undoubtedly read into this prolonged tête-à-tête by the movie colony, whose greatest indoor game is to create imaginary infidelities. In this case, however, what they didn't know was that Marilyn had come to the dinner with a list of questions on civil rights that she planned to press upon a friendly politician. It's a delicious thought: carnality in the eye of the beholder, civil rights in the hushed voices of Bobby and Marilyn.

She admired the Kennedys; she admired youth and flair. During a fund-raising dinner dance for the Democratic Party in Los Angeles that Marilyn attended, she told of dancing with Robert Kennedy, then attorney general in the Cabinet. "He was very nice, sort of boyish and likable. Of course he kept looking down my dress, but I'm used to that. I thought he was going to compliment me, but he asked me while dancing who I thought was the handsomest man in the room. I mean, how was I going to answer that? I said he was. Well, in a way he *was!*"

This handsome dancing partner was to suffer the same fate as his brother. A chain of death forming, a mysterious bond of destiny.

Marilyn's unauthorized visit to New York, not to mention the political implications of her appearance, seemed to stretch the patience of the studio beyond repair. This was complicated (again!) by her weakening physical condition. Added to her anxieties was the fact that her analyst was in Europe on vacation. Even though he had placed her in the care of a fellow analyst, she panicked. Dr. Greenson flew back from Europe and urged the studio to give him a week to get her back into shape. The executives agreed, but on the next day (June 7), without warning, she was fired. The other shoe had finally fallen; it was heard round the world.

Shortly after, when the film was shelved, comment appeared in the local press, with rumors of her coworkers bitterly blaming Marilyn for taking away their jobs. This reaction deeply wounded her. She had always felt a strong kinship with working people, from the taxi driver to the grip man on the set; she felt they were her friends, and now they were publicly accusing her of betraying them. Those whom she trusted, the media people who always defended her, were ready to dethrone her. Marilyn was down, the count had begun.

And finally, that other circle closing, our private joke, our old pact of one calling the other if either were going to jump. She phoned on August 4, 1962, the day before her death. Was that the call, I have often thought, the one I was ready for? Perhaps it was, but too heavily disguised for me to decipher. On the surface, a cheerful, excited conversation. Had we seen her *Life* interview that had just come out? We did, we told her it was great, we liked the spirit. She talked about the future—was that a hint?—and how excited she was about coming East in a month or so. "We'll go down to Washington together," she said. "I'm invited to a benefit performance of a new musical at the end of September, box seats, the works. We'll

have a great time, we have to start living, right?"
High, bubbly, optimistic—was that the call I didn't
recognize? I wasn't listening hard enough. She
spoke of her house, almost completed; the Mexican
tile was in, the furnishings were finally about to
arrive. And her garden—how beautiful it was going
to be, new shrubs and trees. She raced from one
subject to another. "Look, why don't you both
come out and stay for a while? I miss you. Please
come. I'll get the pool warmed up. If you both
can't come now, how about Hedda alone? And
how is everybody at home? Sure you're all right?
And Pat, is she having a nice summer? I haven't
seen her for ages. Give her my love. And how are
you both?" Marilyn didn't often ask how we were,
not that insistently. "By the way, the picture may
still be done. Besides, I've had offers from all over
the world. Yes, wonderful offers but I'm not thinking about them yet." Barely a pause. There was
something in code, a message I couldn't quite
decipher flashing out from beneath the lines. The
message was: Help. She chatted on, "Let's all start
to live before we get old, and how are you and all
the girls and how are you *really* and you're sure
everything is all right. . . . ? Listen, I have to hang
up, got a long distance call on the line. I'll speak to
you on Monday. G'bye."

She fooled me. She didn't say she was going to
do it—or didn't she know then? She made a last
call to somebody. It wasn't to me.

Recently, I came across a letter in my desk addressed to Marilyn Monroe, 12305 Fifth Helena Drive, Los Angeles 49, California. Postmark: August 4, 11:30 P.M., 1962. It was a letter I had written to her the day of her last call. It was never opened. She died in the early morning hours of August 6, 1962, before it arrived.

When the letter was returned, I felt then it was part of a closed history, a postscript to a tragedy. Yet I could not destroy it—my last personal link to a remarkable person. It remained sealed, deliberately set aside. Years later, I opened the envelope and read what I had written.

Dear Marilyn, following up on my quick postcard, this is to say that my second thoughts on your *Life* interview are as good as my first. Why were you so worried over the phone? Relax. I re-read it, and what you say is sensitive, meaningful and honest. And courageous, too. You looked the world in the eye and spoke your piece. You let the world know you could evaluate your life as much as anyone could. Our poet friend Ettore said he enjoyed it, too. He said you owed him a letter, by the way. I said to him, You're not supposed to get Marilyn's letters by mail, you're supposed to *feel* them. Well, anyway, *I* do. Don't be mad I never swam in your

pool on my last visit. We look forward to
seeing you in September.

'And there was that blind moment of fear during those hours of August 6 when the nonperson
overwhelmed her, she reached for the pills, and
September never came for her.

Many have spoken since then. From Hollywood
and New York and points around the world,
agents, directors, admirers ("She was great, magical"), detractors ("I'd rather do my next film
with Hitler"), leading men (domestic and foreign), documentary researchers, Time & Life,
novelists, playwrights, ex-husbands, sociologists,
drama coaches, psychiatrists friendly and hostile,
columnists who made it up out of whole cloth, bi-
ographers who had the pieces but never the real
thing, fantasists, phonies, bleeding hearts—they
all "knew" her.

But she has escaped the facts and flown into
myth, caught in a twilight of blended history and
remembrance. She haunts us with questions that
can never be answered. All beauty is mystery.
What comes back to us is the smile, the desperate
heart, the image that flares up and will not go
away.

In my desk is another reminder I sometimes
glance at. It's a postcard she had sent me once upon
a time. On one side, an American Airlines jet in

flight. On the other, the message, a single sentence: "Guess where I am? Love, Marilyn."

> Who killed Norma Jean?
>   I, said the City,
>   As a civic duty
> I killed Norma Jean.
>
> Who saw her die?
>   I, said the Night,
>   And a bedroom light,
> We saw her die.
>
> Who caught her blood?
>   I, said the Fan,
>   With my little pan,
> I caught her blood.
>
> Who'll make her shroud?
>   I, said her Lover,
>   My guilt to cover,
> I'll make her shroud.
>
> Who'll dig her grave?
>   The Tourist will come
>   To join in the fun.
> He'll dig her grave.
>
> Who'll be chief mourners?
>   We who represent
>   And lose our ten percent,
> We'll be chief mourners.

Who'll bear the pall?
　We, said the Press,
　In pain and distress
We'll bear the pall.

Who'll toll the bell?
　I, screamed the Mother,
　Locked in her tower,
I'll pull the bell.

Who'll soon forget?
　I, said the Page,
　Beginning to fade,
I'm first to forget.

Big Bestsellers from SIGNET

☐ **TO REACH A DREAM by Nathan C. Heard.** From the author of the bestselling **Howard Street** comes a seething new novel of streetcorner manhood at the bottom of a black ghetto. "Raw, brutal, memorable."—**The New York Times** (#Y5490—$1.25)

☐ **THE SEX SURROGATES by Michael Davidson.** The raw tapes of the sex clinic—a startling novel about the men and women—strangers—who find themselves partners in love. (#Y5410—$1.25)

☐ **AN OLD-FASHIONED DARLING by Charles Simmons.** Can a young man who works on a sex magazine and has a harem of sexually voracious ladies, break the sex habit? "Unrestrained delight."—**The New York Times** (#Q5355—95¢)

☐ **THE WHITE DAWN by James Houston.** Three white men are rescued from a shipwreck by an isolated Eskimo tribe and are allowed to live with the natives. This is the story of what happened as two alien cultures moved inexorably on a collision course . . . "A vivid, boiling adventure of savage excitement and sensual delights . . . powerful and beautiful."—**Chicago Sun-Times** (#Y5280—$1.25)

☐ **GOLDENROD by Herbert Harker. Goldenrod** is about love in its widest, deepest meaning, and like love, it is both funny and serious, joyous and sad, and very beautiful. "One of the most enchanting novels ever written. . . ."—Ross Macdonald, **New York Times Book Review** (#Y5487—$1.25)

THE NEW AMERICAN LIBRARY, INC.,
P.O. Box 999, Bergenfield, New Jersey 07621

Please send me the SIGNET BOOKS I have checked above. I am enclosing $_____(check or money order—no currency or C.O.D.'s). Please include the list price plus 25¢ a copy to cover handling and mailing costs. (Prices and numbers are subject to change without notice.)

Name_____

Address_____

City_____State_____Zip Code_____
Allow at least 3 weeks for delivery

More Bestsellers from SIGNET

☐ **WOULD YOU BELIEVE LOVE?** by Eliza McCormack. If there's an over-thirty lady who can read this and not laugh and cry and rage, she'll be hard to find. "Enchanting . . ."—**Boston Globe** (#Y5197—$1.25)

☐ **TO SMITHEREENS by Rosalyn Drexler.** A heartwarming love story with the kick of a karate chop. . . . "If Lenny Bruce had written a novel, this would have been it!" —Jack Newfield (#Q5281—95¢)

☐ **THE CENTER by Charles Beardsley.** From the author of **The Motel** comes a torrid new novel of scorching sex and warped desires among therapists who cannot cure their own devastating lusts. (#Y5653—$1.25)

☐ **THE MUGGING by Morton Hunt.** From the bestselling author of **The Affair** comes the anatomy of a mugging— the sudden savage assault by a stranger who leaps from the shadows. "Touches a raw nerve."—**New York Daily News** (#E5509—$1.75)

☐ **THE PATROLMAN: A COP'S STORY by Edward F. Droge, Jr.** A shattering book that takes you into the squad cars, the precinct houses, the alleyways—and into a policeman's very guts! (#Y5468—$1.25)

☐ **THE PRIVATE SECTOR by Joseph Hone.** A brilliant and calculated spy story of callous political and human intrigue—double and triple agents on the London-Moscow circuit, denizens of the dark alleyways of Cairo during the weeks leading up to the Six-Day War. "Absolutely chilling, enthralling."—**Boston Globe** (#Y5463—$1.25)

THE NEW AMERICAN LIBRARY, INC.,
P.O. Box 999, Bergenfield, New Jersey 07621

Please send me the SIGNET BOOKS I have checked above. I am enclosing $_____(check or money order—no currency or C.O.D.'s). Please include the list price plus 25¢ a copy to cover handling and mailing costs. (Prices and numbers are subject to change without notice.)

Name_____

Address_____

City_____State_____Zip Code_____
Allow at least 3 weeks for delivery

Have You Read These Bestsellers from SIGNET?

☐ **BRING ME A UNICORN: The Diaries and Letters of Anne Morrow Lindbergh (1922–1928) by Anne Morrow Lindbergh.** Imagine being loved by the most worshipped hero on Earth. This nationally acclaimed bestseller is the chronicle of just such a love. The hero was Charles Lindbergh: the woman he loved was Anne Morrow Lindbergh; and the story of their love was one of the greatest romances of any time. "Extraordinary . . . brings to intense life every moment as she lived it."—**New York Times Book Review** (#W5352—$1.50)

☐ **ELEANOR AND FRANKLIN by Joseph P. Lash.** Foreword by Arthur M. Schlesinger, Jr. A number 1 bestseller and winner of the Pulitzer Prize and the National Book Award, this is the intimate chronicle of Eleanor Roosevelt and her marriage to Franklin D. Roosevelt, with its painful secrets and public triumphs. "An exceptionally candid, exhaustive . . . heartrending book."—**The New Yorker** (#J5310—$1.95)

☐ **JENNIE, VOLUME I: The Life of Lady Randolph Churchill by Ralph G. Martin.** In JENNIE, Ralph G. Martin creates a vivid picture of an exciting woman, Lady Randolph Churchill, who was the mother of perhaps the greatest statesman of this century, Winston Churchill, and in her own right, one of the most colorful and fascinating women of the Victorian era. (#E5229—$1.75)

☐ **JENNIE, VOLUME II: The Life of Lady Randolph Churchill, the Dramatic Years 1895–1921 by Ralph G. Martin.** The climactic years of scandalous passion and immortal greatness of the American beauty who raised a son to shape history, Winston Churchill. "An extraordinary lady . . . if you couldn't put down JENNIE ONE, you'll find JENNIE TWO just as compulsive reading!"—**Washington Post** (#E5196—$1.75)

THE NEW AMERICAN LIBRARY, INC.,
P.O. Box 999, Bergenfield, New Jersey 07621

Please send me the SIGNET BOOKS I have checked above. I am enclosing $_____(check or money order—no currency or C.O.D.'s). Please include the list price plus 25¢ a copy to cover handling and mailing costs. (Prices and numbers are subject to change without notice.)

Name_____

Address_____

City_____State_____Zip Code_____
Allow at least 3 weeks for delivery